# AN EVENT-BASED SCIENCE MODULE

# GOLD RUSH!

## STUDENT EDITION

## Russell G. Wright

Dale Seymour Publications®

The developers of Event-Based Science (EBS) have been encouraged and supported at every step in the creative process by the superintendent and board of education of Montgomery County Public Schools, Rockville, Maryland (MCPS). The superintendent and board are committed to the systemic improvement of science instruction, grades preK–12. EBS is one of many projects undertaken to ensure the scientific literacy of all students.

The developers of *Gold Rush!* pay special tribute to the editors, publisher, and reporters of *USA Today*. Without their cooperation and support, the creation of this module would not have been possible.

Photographs: pages 5, 6, 8, 12, 13, 21, 45, California Department of Parks and Recreation; page 17, Kennecott Corporation; page 23, Joe Brilla; pages 43, 44, Mineral Policy Center; pages 48 bottom, 49 bottom, 50 bottom, NASA; page 48 top, EOSAT; page 49 top, Pamela Lee, NASA; page 50 top, Lockheed Missiles and Space Co.; and all "Student Voices" photographs by Charles E. Doebler.

Managing Editor: Cathy Anderson

Project Editor: Lois Fowkes

Production and Manufacturing: Leanne Collins

Design Manager: Jeff Kelly

Text and Cover Design: Frank Loose Design

Cover Photograph: ©1989 Wm Whitehurst, The Stock Market

This book is published by Dale Seymour Publications®, an imprint of Addison Wesley Longman, Inc.

This material is based on work supported by the National Science Foundation under grant number MDR-9154094. Any opinions, findings, conclusions, or recommendations expressed in this publication are those of the Event-Based Science Project and do not necessarily reflect the views of the National Science Foundation.

Printed in the United States of America.

Order Number DS30684
ISBN 0-201-49599-6

DALE
SEYMOUR
PUBLICATIONS®
P.O. BOX 10888
PALO ALTO, CA 94303

This product is printed
on recycled paper

6 7 8 9 10 11-ML-06 05 04 03 02 01

# Contents

**On the Job**

**Interdisciplinary Activities**

**Performance Assessment**

# Preface

## The Event-Based Science Model

*Gold Rush!* is an earth-science module that follows the Event-Based Science (EBS) instructional model. You will watch a televised recreation of the 1848 discovery of gold in California. You will also read newspaper accounts of the Gold Rush. Your discussions about the Gold Rush will show you and your teacher that you already know a lot about the earth-science concepts involved in the event. Next, a real-world Task puts you and your classmates in the roles of people who must use scientific knowledge and processes to solve problems related to gold and other valuable minerals. You will probably need more information before you start the Task. If you do, *Gold Rush!* provides hands-on activities and a variety of reading materials to give you some of the background you need. About halfway through the module, you will be ready to begin the Task. Your teacher will assign you a role to play and turn you and your team loose to complete the Task. You will spend the rest of the time in this module working on the Task.

## Scientific Literacy

A literate citizen is expected to know more than how to read, write, and do simple arithmetic. Today, literacy includes knowing how to analyze problems, ask critical questions, and explain events. A literate citizen must also be able to apply scientific knowledge and processes to new situations. Event-Based Science allows you to practice these skills by placing the study of science in a meaningful context.

Knowledge cannot be transferred to your mind from the mind of your teacher nor from the pages of a textbook. Neither can knowledge occur in isolation from the other things you know about and have experienced in the real world. The Event-Based Science model is based on the idea that the best way to know something is to be actively engaged in it.

Therefore, the Event-Based Science model simulates real-life events and experiences to make your learning more authentic and memorable. First, the event is brought to life through a television documentary. Viewing the documentary allows you to be there "as it happened," and that is as close as you can get to actually experiencing the event. Second, by simulating the kinds of teamwork and problem solving that occur every day in our work places and communities, you will experience the role that scientific knowledge and teamwork play in the lives of ordinary people. Thus *Gold Rush!* is built around simulations of real-life events and experiences that affected people's lives and environments dramatically.

In an Event-Based Science classroom, you become the workers; your product is a solution to a real problem; and your teacher is your coach, guide, and advisor. You will be assessed on how you use scientific processes and concepts to solve problems as well as on the quality of your work.

One of the primary goals of the Event-Based Science Project is to place the learning of science in a real-world context and to make scientific learning fun. You should not allow yourself to become frustrated. If you cannot find a specific piece of information, it's okay to be creative. For example, if you are working as the geologist and you cannot find information about the site, base your response on the real places and things you know about. Just remember to identify your creations as fictional.

## Student Resources

*Gold Rush!* is unlike a regular textbook. An Event-Based Science module tells a story about a real event; it has real newspaper articles about the event and inserts that explain the scientific concepts involved in the event. It also contains Science Activities for you to conduct in your science class and Interdisciplinary Activities that you may do in language arts, math, social studies, or technology education classes. In addition, an Event-Based Science module gives you and your classmates a real-world Task to do. The Task is always done by teams of students, with each team member performing a real-life role while completing an important part of the Task. The Task cannot be completed unless you and everyone else on your team do your parts. The team approach allows you to share your knowledge and strengths. It also helps you learn to work with a team in a real-world situation. Today, most professionals work in teams.

Interviews with people who actually serve in the roles you are playing are scattered throughout the Event-Based Science module. Middle-school students who actually experienced panning for gold tell their stories throughout the module, too.

Since this module is unlike a regular textbook, you have much more flexibility in using it.

- You may read **The Story** for enjoyment or to find clues that will help you tackle your part of the Task.
- You may read selections from the **Discovery File** when you need help understanding something in the Story or when you need help with the Task.
- You may read all the **On the Job** features because you are curious about what professionals do, or you may read only the interview with the professional who works in the role you've chosen because it may give you ideas that will help you complete the Task.
- You may read the **In the News** features because they catch your eye or as part of your search for information.

- You will probably read all the **Student Voices** features because they are interesting stories told by middle-school students such as yourself.

*Gold Rush!* is also unlike regular textbooks in that the collection of resources found in it is not meant to be complete. You must find additional information from other sources, too. Textbooks, encyclopedias, pamphlets, magazine and newspaper articles, videos, films, filmstrips, computer databases, the internet, and people in your community are all potential sources of useful information. It is vital to your preparation as a scientifically literate citizen of the twenty-first century that you get used to finding information on your own.

The shape of a new form of science education is beginning to emerge, and the Event-Based Science Project is leading the way. We hope you enjoy your experience with this module as much as we enjoyed developing it.

—Russell G. Wright, Ed.D.
Project Director and Principal Author

# The Quiet Before the Rush

A harsh, cold winter day dawned in California. The date was January 24, 1848. For James Marshall, it was a morning like any other. He strolled through the sawmill he was in charge of building. The mill was taking shape along a branch of the American River in the Sacramento valley. The flow of water was diverted from the river into the mill. It brought with it mud, sand, and gravel.

As he had been doing each morning, Marshall inspected the watercourse. At a shallow spot, he saw something he had never seen before. It glittered with a sun-yellow color. The water was only six inches deep, so Marshall reached in and picked up the tiny piece of material. It was about half the size of a pea. He pulled from the water another piece and pondered what he had discovered.

Marshall took the pebbles to his fellow mill workers. "Boys," Marshall said to his coworkers, "I believe I have found a gold mine!" But at first look, Marshall's workmen laughed off the mysterious substance as nothing more than *fool's gold*—an iron pyrite. Then a worker placed one of the pieces on an anvil and pounded it with a hammer. To everyone's surprise, the yellow matter flattened out. Fool's gold would have shattered.

Then Marshall placed a piece of the metal in a large kettle with baking soda and lye soap and boiled the mixture for a day. The gleaming piece did not change color. Indeed, the material appeared to be as good as gold. But more tests were needed.

A few days later, Marshall rode his horse 50 miles to Sutter's Fort. The sprawling outpost was owned by John Sutter. It was for Sutter, in fact, that the sawmill was being built. Marshall carried with him a rolled-up piece of cotton cloth. It held numerous samples of the sparkling material found at the mill.

Upon arriving, Marshall whisked Sutter into a quiet room of his house. He demanded Sutter lock the door. A confused and concerned Sutter had no idea why Marshall was acting so strangely. Marshall unrolled the cloth and looked at Sutter. Then he told him where it came from—Sutter's mill. But was it the glitter of gold . . . or something else?

Sutter turned to his small library of books. An encyclopedia advised using nitric acid to test for the qualities and properties of gold. Sutter had acid fetched from one of the fort's stores. The men poured the acid onto the metal. They could not see any effect.

They then used a set of small scales. They put silver in one tray and balanced the scales using an equal weight of the yellow metal. Finally, they submerged the two materials in two bowls of water. Being more dense than the silver, the yellow metal quickly sank. Sutter finally believed Marshall. The material was gold. It also appeared that the metal was very pure, with little silver or copper.

Sutter and Marshall quietly agreed it was best to keep the gold find a closely guarded secret.

### STUDENT VOICES

I probably wouldn't have gone west in 1849 to make my fortune in the gold fields of California. Panning for gold is really hard work. It's really long and really tedious.

FRANCELINE STAUDENMANN
NORTH POTOMAC, MD

## Discussion Questions

- **Is gold a rock or a mineral?**

- **Is gold found in your state?**

- **What makes gold valuable?**

- **Name other valuable rocks and minerals that come from the ground.**

- **If someone tried to sell you a bar of pure gold, how could you be sure it was real?**

# What's the Matter?

Atoms are the basic building blocks of matter. Rocks are made of atoms. Air is made of atoms. You are made of atoms, too. Atoms are extremely small. If you stack more than a million atoms on top of each other, the stack would only be as thick as this sheet of paper.

Atoms can occur alone, unattached to other atoms. In other instances atoms interact or join together to form molecules. Two of the same kind of atom can join together. For example, two oxygen atoms (O) can join to form an oxygen molecule.

Sometimes different kinds of atoms exist side by side in an arrangement called a *mixture*. Our atmosphere is mostly a mixture of two elements, nitrogen and oxygen, with a little bit of carbon dioxide ($CO_2$) and pollution mixed in.

In some cases different kinds of atoms join together to form new substances called *compounds*. For example, two atoms of hydrogen (H) can link together with one atom of oxygen (O) to form a molecule of water ($H_2O$). Water is a compound. Its properties are different from the properties of either hydrogen or oxygen.

Hydrogen is a very explosive gas. Oxygen is the element that supports combustion: fires need oxygen to burn. However, when oxygen and hydrogen join together as water, they lose their properties. Water is liquid at room temperature. Water does not burn or support fires; it puts fires out.

More than 2,000 years ago, Greek philosophers gave the atom its name. The *a* means "not" and *tom* means "divide." They thought the atom could not be divided. They described it as the basic building block of everything in the universe. We now know that there is a swarm of activity inside every atom. But atoms are still believed to be the smallest particles to carry the characteristics and properties of the naturally occurring elements.

## The Periodic Table of Elements

Chemistry immerses you in the study of matter. The periodic table of elements is a valuable tool for this adventure. Only substances composed of a single type of atom are listed on this table. Ninety-two such pure substances occur naturally on Earth. Another 17 substances are human made. Whether a pure substance, mixture, or compound, everything in the universe is composed of this same set of elements.

## Reactions Among Elements

Generally speaking, the elements on the left side of the periodic table are metals and the ones on the upper right side are nonmetals. The best known metals are found in the lower center of the table. Metals can react with nonmetals to form compounds. Iron (Fe) slowly reacts with oxygen ($O_2$) to form rust ($Fe_2O_3$). Iron is moderately reactive.

Gold is a metallic element that does not form compounds easily. That is why gold does not tarnish. It keeps its bright and shiny appearance without polishing. Gold atoms are not very reactive.

The metal sodium (Na), on the other hand, is so reactive it reacts explosively with water.

---

**IN THE NEWS**

The following was taken from the *Weekly Pacific News* in San Francisco, Friday, March 1, 1850.

"People who come to California to make money by mining, should be prepared for the hardships of a mountain life, and not only possess good constitutions, but avoid the dissipations which are too frequently the cause of a greater portion of the sickness that has given the mining sections of the country their reputations for unhealthiness.

"We can do without the class of good-for-nothing, thriftless fellows, who won't work at home, but who think if they can only get to California their fortune is sure to be made in a few months. Men of nerve and industry will here, as every where else, be successful; and as to health, no one with a good constitution and using common prudence need fear sickness in this country more than in the States. We deem California, in every respect, as healthy as any equal extent of territory on the face of the globe."

| PERIOD | 1 1A | 2 2A | 3 3B | 4 4B | 5 5B | 6 6B | 7 7B | 8 8B | 9 8B | 10 | 11 1B | 12 2B | 13 3A | 14 4A | 15 5A | 16 6A | 17 7A | 18 8A |
|---|---|---|---|---|---|---|---|---|---|---|---|---|---|---|---|---|---|---|
| 1 | 1 **H** 1.00794 | | | | | | | | | | | | | | | | | 2 **He** 4.00260 |
| 2 | 3 **Li** 6.941 | 4 **Be** 9.01218 | | | | | | | | | | | 5 **B** 10.811 | 6 **C** 12.011 | 7 **N** 14.0067 | 8 **O** 15.9994 | 9 **F** 18.9984 | 10 **Ne** 20.1797 |
| 3 | 11 **Na** 22.9898 | 12 **Mg** 24.3050 | | | | | | | | | | | 13 **Al** 26.9815 | 14 **Si** 28.0855 | 15 **P** 30.9738 | 16 **S** 32.066 | 17 **Cl** 35.4527 | 18 **Ar** 39.948 |
| 4 | 19 **K** 39.0983 | 20 **Ca** 40.078 | 21 **Sc** 44.9559 | 22 **Ti** 47.88 | 23 **V** 50.9415 | 24 **Cr** 51.9961 | 25 **Mn** 54.9381 | 26 **Fe** 55.847 | 27 **Co** 58.9332 | 28 **Ni** 58.69 | 29 **Cu** 63.546 | 30 **Zn** 65.39 | 31 **Ga** 69.723 | 32 **Ge** 72.61 | 33 **As** 74.9216 | 34 **Se** 78.96 | 35 **Br** 79.904 | 36 **Kr** 83.80 |
| 5 | 37 **Rb** 85.4678 | 38 **Sr** 87.62 | 39 **Y** 88.9059 | 40 **Zr** 91.224 | 41 **Nb** 92.9064 | 42 **Mo** 95.94 | 43 **Tc** (98) | 44 **Ru** 101.07 | 45 **Rh** 102.906 | 46 **Pd** 106.42 | 47 **Ag** 107.868 | 48 **Cd** 112.411 | 49 **In** 114.82 | 50 **Sn** 118.710 | 51 **Sb** 121.75 | 52 **Te** 127.60 | 53 **I** 126.904 | 54 **Xe** 131.29 |
| 6 | 55 **Cs** 132.905 | 56 **Ba** 137.327 | 57 ***La** 138.906 | 72 **Hf** 178.49 | 73 **Ta** 180.948 | 74 **W** 183.85 | 75 **Re** 186.207 | 76 **Os** 190.2 | 77 **Ir** 192.22 | 78 **Pt** 195.08 | 79 **Au** 196.967 | 80 **Hg** 200.59 | 81 **Tl** 204.383 | 82 **Pb** 207.2 | 83 **Bi** 208.980 | 84 **Po** (209) | 85 **At** (210) | 86 **Rn** (222) |
| 7 | 87 **Fr** (223) | 88 **Ra** 226.025 | 89 †**Ac** 227.028 | 104 **Unq** (261) | 105 **Unp** (262) | 106 **Unh** (263) | 107 **Uns** (262) | 108 **Uno** (265) | 109 **Une** (266) | | | | | | | | | |

*Lanthanide series:

| 58 **Ce** 140.115 | 59 **Pr** 140.908 | 60 **Nd** 144.24 | 61 **Pm** (145) | 62 **Sm** 150.36 | 63 **Eu** 151.965 | 64 **Gd** 157.25 | 65 **Tb** 158.925 | 66 **Dy** 162.50 | 67 **Ho** 164.930 | 68 **Er** 167.26 | 69 **Tm** 168.934 | 70 **Yb** 173.04 | 71 **Lu** 174.967 |
|---|---|---|---|---|---|---|---|---|---|---|---|---|---|

†Actinide series:

| 90 **Th** 232.038 | 91 **Pa** 231.036 | 92 **U** 238.029 | 93 **Np** 237.048 | 94 **Pu** (244) | 95 **Am** (243) | 96 **Cm** (247) | 97 **Bk** (247) | 98 **Cf** (251) | 99 **Es** (252) | 100 **Fm** (257) | 101 **Md** (258) | 102 **No** (259) | 103 **Lr** (260) |
|---|---|---|---|---|---|---|---|---|---|---|---|---|---|

# Mineral Characteristics

Minerals occur naturally. They are solids. They are made of regular, repeating arrangements of atoms and molecules, which produce their characteristic crystal shapes.

Valuable minerals are found in very small amounts in all soils and rocks. A mineral deposit is a concentration of the mineral large enough to have economic value. A good place to find mineral deposits is in a mountain or deep underground.

Two important characteristics of minerals are hardness and specific gravity.

## Hardness

The hardness of a mineral is its resistance to scratching. A mineral's hardness can be described relative to a standard scale of ten minerals known as the Mohs scale. Austrian mineralogist Friedrich Mohs developed this scale in 1822. Talc is the softest mineral on the scale at 1. Diamonds are the hardest at 10.

### Mohs Scale

| | |
|---|---|
| Talc | 1 |
| Gypsum | 2 |
| Calcite | 3 |
| Fluorite | 4 |
| Apatite | 5 |
| Feldspar | 6 |
| Quartz | 7 |
| Topaz | 8 |
| Sapphire | 9 |
| Diamond | 10 |

## Specific Gravity

Specific gravity is the number of times heavier a gemstone of any volume is than an equal volume of water. In other words, specific gravity is the ratio of the density of a gemstone to the density of water. The specific gravity of diamond is 3.52. This means a diamond is about three and a half times heavier than the same volume of water. Measurement of specific gravity can be used to help confirm the identity of a mineral.

The Task for *Gold Rush!* offers you a choice of mining gold, silver, copper, diamonds, or limestone. Additional information about these minerals is easily available in libraries, through on-line services, and from government agencies such as the U.S. Geological Survey and U.S. Bureau of Mines. You may come across unfamiliar words in the following text, so be sure to look them up!

## Gold

**Periodic Table Symbol:** Au

**Atomic Number:** 79 (Atomic number is the number of protons in the atoms of an element.

**Luster:** Metallic

**Hardness:** 2.5 to 3

**Specific Gravity:** 19.3 (This means gold is 19.3 times heavier than the same volume of water.)

**Tests:** Gold fuses easily on charcoal, forming golden buttons. Pure gold is soluble in aqua regia; silver-rich gold is soluble in other acids.

**Environment:** Gold is found in quartz veins and stream deposits.

**Crystal Description:** Gold usually has octahedral (eight-sided) crystals with or without additional faces. Clusters of gold crystals commonly grow parallel to each other. They are often distorted into the shape of feathery leaves, wires, or thin plates.

**Occurrences:** Gold occurs widely, originating most often in quartz or sulfide veins. Gold also concentrates in stream beds. This is because of its great density and inertness. It is found in the form of small flakes or larger nuggets that can be recovered by panning. Gold is also found in brown, iron-stained rock. Weathering frees the gold from the rock. Nuggets become more rounded the farther they have traveled from their source.

**Uses:** Gold is used for jewelry, coins, medicine, electronics, and dentistry, to name a few applications. Space travel depends on gold. Gold reflects heat for firefighters, satellites, and astronauts.

## Silver

**Periodic Table Symbol:** Ag

**Atomic Number:** 47

**Luster:** Metallic

**Hardness:** 2.5 to 3

**Specific Gravity:** 10.0 to 11.0 (This means silver is 10 to 11 times heavier than the same volume of water.)

**Tests:** Pure silver fuses easily on charcoal, forming white buttons, or disks. Impurities tend to make melting more difficult.

Silver dissolves in nitric acid and changes to a curdy appearance when hydrochloric acid is added.

**Environment:** Silver is found in ore veins.

**Crystal Description:** Silver crystals mainly form long, distorted wires, sometimes in cubic or octahedral crystals.

**Occurrences:** Silver is found with other metals, including gold, copper, lead, and zinc. Approximately 80 percent of the silver mined today is a byproduct of mining and processing these other metals.

**Uses:** In addition to jewelry and silverware, silver is used in dental fillings and photographic film. It is also used in the contacts of wall-mounted light switches and numerous electrical appliances. Silver is used to prevent the buildup of bacteria and algae in water-purifier filters. It is also used in cars and spacecraft, including the space shuttles.

## Copper

**Periodic Table Symbol:** Cu

**Atomic Number:** 29

**Luster:** Metallic

**Hardness:** 2.5 to 3

**Specific Gravity:** 8.9 (This means copper is 8.9 times heavier than the same volume of water.)

**Tests:** Small bits of copper fuse on charcoal, making black-coated copper buttons. Copper is soluble in acids, making greenish solutions. When burned, copper compounds make a blue-green flame.

**Environment:** Copper occurs in copper sulfide veins and in some types of volcanic rock.

**Crystal Description:** Copper is usually in distorted, rounded, complex crystals in the shape of cubes, octahedrons (8-sided solids), and dodecahedrons (12-sided solids). It is often found in masses without recognizable crystal forms.

**Occurrences:** Native copper is found in ancient lava flows.

**Uses:** Because it is an excellent conductor of heat and electricity, copper is used extensively in electrical wiring and appliances, cars, and computers. Along with other minerals, copper is also important in our diet for good nutrition.

**Copper Alloys:** When a metal is combined with one or more other metals, it is called an *alloy*. Brass is an alloy of copper and zinc. Copper combines with tin to make bronze.

## Diamond

**Periodic Table Element:** Carbon (in crystalline form)

**Periodic Table Symbol:** C

**Atomic Number:** 6

**Luster:** Greasy (low-quality diamonds)

**Hardness:** 10 (hardest)

**Specific Gravity:** 3.52 (This means diamond is 3.52 times heavier than the same volume of water.)

**Tests:** Diamonds are infusible and insoluble. They burn at high temperatures.

**Environment:** Diamond is found in alluvial deposits usually derived from dark igneous rock. It is also in kimberlite, found at the core of a volcano. The richest diamond deposits are found in kimberlite pipes in Africa.

**Crystal Description:** Diamond is most often octahedral. Each atom in a diamond is bonded to four other atoms in a tetrahedral (10-sided) arrangement, which accounts for its hardness.

➤ continued on page 6

*Miners working a stream.* PHOTO FROM THE CALIFORNIA DEPARTMENT OF PARKS AND RECREATION.

**Occurrences:** In alluvial deposits, the harder and heavier diamonds have survived when the parent rock has weathered and worn away. Diamonds are mined from their original rocks only in South Africa, Siberia, and Arkansas.

**Uses:**
Diamond is the hardest natural substance known. Diamonds are not only valued for jewelry; they are also highly valued for industrial purposes such as rock drills, turning tools, and abrasive powder.

Much of the diamond that is mined is not gem quality. Because of this, the average diamond in an engagement ring is the result of removing and processing of a huge amount of rock—about 200 to 400 million times the volume, or size, of the diamond itself.

## Calcite

**Periodic Table Compound:** Calcite, also known as calcium carbonate ($CaCO_3$)

**Periodic Table Symbols:** Ca (calcium), C (carbon), and O (oxygen)

**Atomic Numbers:** 20 (calcium), 6 (carbon), and 8 (oxygen)

**Luster:** Glassy

**Hardness:** 3 (cleavage face)

**Specific Gravity:** 2.7 (This means calcite is 2.7 times heavier than the same volume of water.)

**Tests:** Calcite is easily scratched and dissolves in cold, diluted hydrochloric acid with effervescence.

**Environment:** Calcite occurs everywhere, within all classes of rocks.

**Crystal Description:** Calcite is often crystallized. It has an extremely varied appearance, from tabular (which is rare) to prismatic or needle-like. Its size varies from microcrystalline to coarse. The coarse crystal is called *limestone*.

**Occurrences:** Calcite is one of the most common minerals. It can form in beds as limestone and in veins. Limestone holds the largest reservoirs of the element carbon at or near the earth's surface. Limestone often contains fossils. It is a sedimentary rock formed by animal remains and other minerals deposited on the sea floor.

**Uses:** Calcite is used as construction materials for buildings and roads. It is also used in glue, paper, soap, and medicine. Limestone also prevents chewing gum from sticking to your teeth.

*Miners on a track.* PHOTO FROM THE CALIFORNIA DEPARTMENT OF PARKS AND RECREATION.

# Testing Materials

### The Scratch Test

Mineralogists define hardness as the resistance of a material to being scratched. A scratch is a small groove cut into the surface of a solid.

When something is scratched, bonds between its atoms are broken. Resistance to being scratched depends on the strength of atomic bonds, so hardness gives us clues about the atomic structure of materials.

The standard test for hardness involves scratching one mineral with another. A mineral is considered harder than the other minerals it can scratch.

The Mohs scale on page 4 lists the hardness of some common minerals. They are listed in order of their increasing hardness. A mineral with a higher hardness number will scratch any mineral with a lower number. Diamond (10) is the hardest natural substance and will scratch any other mineral.

Some common materials useful in testing hardness include your fingernail, with a Mohs-scale value 2.5; a copper penny (3–4 on the scale); a knife blade (5.5 on the scale); window glass (5.5 on the scale); and a steel file (6.5 on the scale).

### The Luster Test

The luster test is a visual assessment of the way the mineral's surface reflects light. The luster of a mineral generally falls into one of two classes: metallic and nonmetallic.

Luster can vary within a single mineral. Luster also varies depending on the direction from which you view the mineral.

Luster does not affect the color of a mineral, except in the case of metals. A metallic mineral really looks metallic, and its color is constant throughout.

Nonmetallic lusters are classified as follows. Examples are in parentheses.

- Vitreous: the luster of glass (quartz)

- Resinous: the luster of resin (amber)

- Greasy: as if covered with a layer of grease or oil (serpentine, some quartz)

- Pearly: the iridescent sheen of mother-of-pearl (talc, mica)

- Silky: the lustrous, fibrous sheen of rayon or silk (fibrous gypsum, asbestos)

- Adamantine: the hard, brilliant flash of a diamond (diamond, corundum—ruby, sapphire)

- Dull: a surface showing little reflectivity (leucite)

- Earthy: the powdery, crumbly look of compacted soil (kaolin clay)

# Bats Help Assess Abandoned Mines

When you find bats inside an abandoned mine, what does that tell you? It means the air quality is good enough to support life in that section of the mine. This helps when you are assessing the levels of possible contamination. It also tells assessors it is probably safe for them to be inside.

Finding bats creates a concern as well. Some species are threatened or endangered. Environmentally responsible mining companies are committed to protecting bats. If there are just a few bats, people will wait until the bats leave the mine after dark before mining. Then they put a tarp over the entrance and fill that section with soil material.

Abandoned mine shafts are a curiosity and sometimes attract people. Your company needs to protect its liability. Remember, public and employee health and safety as well as environmental issues are priorities.

# Mining: How Does It Affect You?

How does mining impact your life? You may think of mining as an activity that has little to do with you or your life.

Look around you. What would be left if you took away the products of mining?

The walls would have to go. They are made of sand and gravel mined from quarries. Chemicals and clay in paint are mined, too. There are steel reinforcements in walls, as well. The metal fixtures on your desk and your chair, your classroom chalkboard, and the chalk all contain minerals that are mined.

How about your T-shirt or blouse? Check the label. Is it 50 percent polyester? Gone! Polyester is a plastic (an organic, oil-based product containing mined chemicals). What about cosmetics? They also contain chemicals and clay from mines.

From the casing of your pen to the eyelets on your shoes, products of mining are all around you. Almost everything you see contains some ingredient that has been mined. Only once-living things—such as wood, wool, and cotton—are truly free from a miner's touch. However, many of those once-living things have gone through manufacturing processes that depend on mined minerals.

The products of mining are everywhere. Copper goes into electric and telephone wires, electric motors, generators, and plumbing pipes. There are 42 different minerals in a telephone handset.

Cars contain iron, manganese, chromium, lead, zinc, platinum, copper, and aluminum. Sand, selenium, silicon, soda ash, and other minerals are used in making glass.

Paper can require clay, lime, or sodium sulfate. Minerals such as titanium, lead, and cadmium help give paints their color; talc, mica, and clay help paints last longer.

The processes involved in refining petroleum and in producing textiles, plastics, and fertilizers depend on chemicals made from minerals.

Painters and sculptors use clay, pigments, and marble. Film for movies and still photographs depends on silver. Minerals are used to make cassette tapes, compact discs, and computers.

Clays are used in bricks, dishes, glass, cleaning products, toothpaste, and cosmetics.

Ever since cave dwellers cast the first stone, minerals have provided tools of war. A country's mineral resources have often been the cause of wars, as well.

Minerals take us wherever we want to go—from your favorite mall to the moon. The gold used in the space suits of astronauts and as thin coatings on equipment protects both from the deadly radiation and heat of the sun.

*Panning a stream.* PHOTO FROM THE CALIFORNIA DEPARTMENT OF PARKS AND RECREATION.

# Environmental Manager

**DENISE GALLEGOS
ENVIRONMENTAL MANAGER
OF AUDITS AND COMPLIANCE
SANTA FE PACIFIC GOLD
CORPORATION
ALBUQUERQUE, NEW
MEXICO**

I often play the role of detective at my job. I work for a gold-mining company. When I'm in the field, I search for clues around mines that can reveal chemical contaminants in the soil or water.

My official title is environmental manager of audits and compliance. I make sure our mines—and the mines we consider purchasing—comply with all the environmental laws. This helps ensure health and safety for our employees and the communities nearby or downstream from the mine.

My interest in science started early. I grew up in a historical, "Wild West" town in northern New Mexico. I was always curious about animals. Why do animals act the way they do? My high-school biology teacher fueled that interest. She provided me with a dissecting kit and books. I spent many hours dissecting fish, rats, rabbits—whatever I could find. My grandmother also encouraged my interest in biology. She provided small bottles in which I could collect bees and bugs so I could study them. Today, I have a bachelor's degree in biology.

Northern New Mexico has many coal mines. I've always been interested in mines and

protecting the environment. I still find it fascinating that people can dig holes in the ground, build rooms, and take equipment there to mine for minerals.

Before I worked for Santa Fe Pacific Gold, I was employed by the United States Abandoned Mine Land Bureau. I spent eight years involved in reclaiming or restoring land around abandoned coal and hard-rock mines. I became the bureau chief but, after two years, I wanted to be back in the field. Growing up, I spent a lot of time hunting and fishing in the mountains. I missed the outdoors.

So I went to work for the Santa Fe Pacific Gold Corporation. The company is the fourth-largest producer of gold in North America. We operate the fourth-largest gold mine in North America at Twin Creeks in Nevada. Like most mines, we operate 24 hours a

day, 364 days per year. (We don't mine on Christmas.)

Because of my background in conducting hazard and environmental-site assessments of abandoned mining properties, I was asked to manage Santa Fe's compliance and auditing programs. Mines are heavily regulated by the U.S. government. The government requires companies to audit or check their operations regularly to make sure the workers are following all the environmental regulations. Companies must file their reports so the government knows when they are, or are not, complying with the regulations.

Curiosity is important in pursuing a career in mining or science. To me, science means trying to find the answer to a question. Most of the time, you come up with more questions than answers.

If you are interested in a career in mining, I suggest you focus on good reading and writing skills. Do well in mathematics, biology, and chemistry. Pursue interests in science outside the classroom as well.

I use my chemistry education every day to answer questions such as "Why are certain chemicals hazardous?" You have to know how to read various chemical compounds and understand what they mean. You need some basic knowledge of how they react with water and air.

I also use mathematics every day. You have to calculate how

➤ continued on page 10

➤ continued from page 9

many parts per million of various chemicals can cause problems in water or other substances. For example, consider a chlorinated solvent used for cleaning carburetors and other parts. As few as seven drops of it can contaminate a 55-gallon drum of used oil and make it hazardous.

We use mathematics to estimate the cost of reclamation projects. Say we are budgeting the cost of filling an abandoned mine shaft. We need to figure the number of cubic yards of material needed, how much it will cost per cubic yard, and how many trucks we'll need to transport the material. Sometimes we are estimating how much seed per acre we need to put down. Then we write the required reports on our projects and findings.

I really enjoy going out to old abandoned mines and assessing the environmental hazards. That is when I play detective. Here is a typical day in the field for me: I head out to assess a mine after one of our geologists requests that I inspect the site. I call ahead to have a laboratory ship out an ice chest with sample jars, water containers, and so on. I need these for my chemical analysis.

I take my backpack, my geological pick, and topographical maps and hop into a four-wheel drive vehicle. I like to get started early in the morning, when wildlife is out. I'm usually at the property for several days, taking soil and water samples. Sometimes the job is dangerous. You have to watch for rattlesnakes in some areas. You

have to be aware of what is happening around you all the time.

Then I send my samples to the laboratory for chemical analysis. After that, it's back to the office to write a report of my findings. I try to answer the following questions: Is there contamination in the water or soil? What kinds of liabilities or legal problems could the company have at this site? How hard would it be to obtain permits for reopening the mine? How difficult will the mine be to explore?

Waiting for the chemical analysis of the samples is like waiting to open presents on your birthday. It is very exciting! Sometimes you think you have mill tailings, but you find out it is just sand. Green water that looks bad can come through the analysis clean. You might think another sample is harmless but find that it has high levels of arsenic or lead.

It is also exciting to design ways to deal with the problems we find. This is what I like most about the job. The report I write goes to the other members of the company's team, including the vice president of environmental quality, the project engineer, the hydrologist, geologists, permit people, and exploration people. They need my input to make decisions and to understand what to look for when they start work at the mine.

Mining impacts all of us on a daily basis. We see the results of mining everywhere: from the graphite in our pencils, to the plastic we use, to the desks we sit in, to the cars we drive. Without mining, our world would not be what it is today.

I think of gold as a "romantic" metal. Gold has taken me to some exotic places. My company is international. I recently returned from assessing a mine on the Amazon River in Brazil.

Open-pit mines are impressive engineering feats. The underground mines are equally remarkable from an engineering standpoint. It is amazing to hold an 80-pound bar of gold in your hands and to know what it takes to get it.

## DISCOVERY FILE

# Money Laundering

"In San Francisco, the posh St. Francis Hotel takes money laundering seriously. Until very recently, the St. Francis had a full-time Coin Washer—someone whose responsibility it was to launder guests' coins. When the practice began in 1938, more people used silver than paper dollars; clean coins meant that ladies wouldn't soil their white gloves by handling the tarnished silver. Today, the St. Francis still washes its guests' coins, but with the advent of the credit card, demand is down to about five to ten hours per week."

Source: *Exploring* (magazine of the Exploratorium in San Francisco, Summer, 1994)

# Reopening the Mine

Monday, January 24, 1848, was a day like any other day for James Wilson Marshall. Marshall was the carpenter at Sutter's mill on California's American River. One of his responsibilities was to check the effectiveness of the sluice gate that was built to deepen the river's channel. Deposits at the lower end of the *millrace* (the channel of water flowing through the mill) showed how well the process was working. As he measured the depth of rocks and gravel deposited on this particular day, he noticed something unusual—a couple of shining stones. Marshall had discovered gold.

Few people realized how the discovery of gold at Sutter's mill would impact history. The Gold Rush of 1849 brought at least 50,000 Americans from all walks of life to California. Hundreds of thousands of abandoned pits and mines were left behind by the gold-mining frenzy.

Mining techniques and extraction methods have changed since the 1800s. *Tailings* (processed rocks and gravel that were once left behind by prospectors) can now be mined again. Valuable gold and other minerals can actually be extracted from the waste of closed mines.

Reopening a mine requires careful evaluation. You must consider many questions:

- What minerals are available on site?
- What is the value of those minerals?
- What is the geology of the area?
- How accessible is the area?
- Are there new extraction techniques?
- How safe is the site?
- Can the environment be left in as good or better shape than you found it?

## The Task

The United States Bureau of Mines lists more than 200,000 abandoned and inactive mines in this country. You and several other mining experts have decided to form a mining company. Your specialty will be reopening abandoned mines. Once you are ready to begin the Task, you will have about a week to gather all the information you can find about the mines your company is considering for reopening. What minerals are present? Are there enough minerals left? Are the prices of the minerals high enough? Will demand for the minerals last? Each of you will evaluate a specific part of the information on each mine. You will also consider the environmental impact of mining each site. You must file a Preliminary Environmental Impact Statement with the United States Environmental Protection Agency when you decide which mine you will reopen.

For each mine, you will receive three parts of an Abandoned Mine Land (AML) Inventory Form and core and laboratory test data.

This is a difficult task. Make sure you are ready for the challenge before you start.

## The Roles

Your team will be composed of five experts. Each of you will have individual tasks and team tasks to complete. The job descriptions for each expert role are listed below. You and your team members will submit a prioritized list to your teacher with your role preferences (first choice, second choice, and so on). First choices will be assigned if possible.

## Job Descriptions

*A miner's log cabin.* PHOTO FROM THE CALIFORNIA DEPARTMENT OF PARKS AND RECREATION.

### Mining Production/ Operations Manager

1. Lead the team in selecting a company name, motto, and logo.
2. Analyze the following sections of the AML Inventory Form: Part I, Sections 1, 2, and 3.
3. Plot the locations of each mine on a Nevada state map.
4. Evaluate each location using the following five-point scale.
   0 = The mine is inaccessible.
   1 = The mine is accessible but very remote.
   2 = The mine is accessible but more than 20 miles from a major transportation center.
   3 = The mine is located between 10 and 20 miles from a major transportation center.
   4 = The mine is located 10 miles or less from a major transportation center.
5. Evaluate the mine's ownership using the following three-point scale:
   0 = private or Native American ownership
   1 = state, county, or municipal ownership
   2 = federal ownership
6. Lead your team in the final selection of a mine to reopen. Use the separate ratings compiled by your team to create a composite score for each mine. Be prepared to explain how your team made its final selection.

### Mining Engineer

1. Because you are responsible for designing and building the mine, you are most interested in the facilities already there.

2. Examine the following sections of the AML Inventory Form: Part I, Section 4 (especially years of operation); Part II, Sections 10, 11, 12, and 16; and the map in Part III.
3. Rate the usefulness of each mine's existing facilities using the following five-point scale.
   0 = Facilities remain but buildings must be removed or water must be pumped out.
   1 = No facilities exist on the site.
   2 = Facilities remain but require renovation that will cost approximately 80 percent of the cost of building new facilities. (Facilities are 10 to 20 years old.)
   3 = Facilities can be repaired for approximately 50 percent of the cost of building new facilities. (Facilities are less than 10 years old.)
   4 = Facilities are in excellent condition and ready to be used.

### Geologist

1. Examine box-and-whiskers plots from a laboratory analysis of the minerals present in each mine.
2. Make a list of the minerals found in each mine in order from most abundant to least abundant.
3. Examine the following section of the AML Inventory form: Part I, Section 4 (especially commodities).

4. Use a newspaper listing of commodity prices to obtain recent prices for all minerals present. Do not worry if you cannot find the price of antimony.

5. Rate the mine's profit potential using the following five-point scale.
   0 = The mine is definitely not worth reopening.
   1 = Profit is highly unlikely.
   2 = Not enough evidence exists to determine profitability.
   3 = Profit is highly likely.
   4 = The mine should never have been closed.

6. Once your team has chosen a mine to reopen, use core-drilling data to construct a three-dimensional map of the site.

### Chemist (Metallurgical Engineer)

1. Examine laboratory reports from each mine. The reports will show percentages of each mineral present at nine random locations on the mine property.

2. Use a box-and-whiskers diagram to analyze each mine.

3. Rate each mine based on the data you examine. Use the following five-point scale.
   0 = Site contains less than 1 percent commercial minerals.
   1 = Site contains 1 to 2 percent commercial minerals.
   2 = Site contains 3 to 4 percent commercial minerals.
   3 = Site contains 4 to 5 percent commercial minerals.
   4 = Site contains more than 5 percent commercial minerals.

4. Provide a brief history of the mineral and its current and future uses for the type of mine your team selects for reopening.

### Environmental Hazards Manager

1. Evaluate each site in terms of its potential for harming the natural environment. Use the following five-point scale.
   0 = Mine is not worth reopening due to existing problems.
   1 = Significant environmental concerns exist.
   2 = Moderate concern exists.
   3 = Some concern exists.
   4 = Little or no environmental concern.

2. Pay particular attention to the following sections of the AML Inventory Form: Part I, Section 5; and Part II, Sections 1, 2, 3, 4, 5, and 13.

3. Lead your team in the preparation of a Preliminary Environmental Impact Statement for the mine your team selects for reopening. This statement should include a brief description of your plan for preventing environmental damage and cleaning up any physical damage that may occur as a result of your mining operation.

PHOTO FROM THE CALIFORNIA DEPARTMENT OF PARKS AND RECREATION.

# It's All in the Name

## Purpose

To create a name, logo, and motto for your mining business and to display them on business cards and a banner.

## Background

You and your colleagues are starting a mining company. You realize any successful business needs a good name, logo, and motto. The ones you select should relate to the job your company does and the positive image you want to portray. Remember, your name, logo, and motto will be among the first things people see when they meet with you and your company. First impressions are lasting ones.

BIG MOOSE MINING COMPANY
*A company worth its salt*

Hugh G. Pitt
manager

1-800-WE-DIGIT

12345 Antler Road
Doo Dad, TX 54321

## Materials

**Per group:**

• Sample business cards

• Colored pencils

• Tagboard, poster board, or cloth 11 by 14 in. or larger

• Tagboard or index cards cut to business-card size

## Procedure

1. Brainstorm with your team to create a company name, logo, and motto.

2. Make a business banner, sign, or flag on 11-by-14 in. or larger cloth, poster board or tagboard. Include the business name, logo, and motto you have selected. The name and/or characteristics of the mineral you plan to mine must be included in some way. For example, if you are mining gold, you might want to put a gold nugget on your sign or flag.

3. Each member of the team should design a business card that shows her or his name and the company name, address, phone number, logo, and motto.

## Conclusion

Display your business sign on the wall near your team.

# So You've Struck Gold

Once you find gold, what do you do next? The first thing to do is stake a claim. Staking a claim means you have a temporary right to mine in that area. But hold on: don't bring your pick, shovel, and wheelbarrow just yet. There are a number of legal matters to consider.

If you are on federal land, you must first find out whether you are in an area that is off limits to mining. Some regions have been designated *wilderness areas.* Opening a new mine in a wilderness area is not permitted.

Finding gold on state-owned land means dealing with state authorities. States have different laws about mining. You may want to find out what the mining laws in your state are.

What if you find gold on privately owned land—land owned by a person or a company? Can you stake a claim? You first must negotiate an agreement with the landowner, who will probably want a percentage of the gold you remove. Be sure to work out all the details in advance, otherwise there are sure to be misunderstandings later. Once you

have reached an agreement, you will both sign a contract (a legal document that states every detail of the agreement).

Also, before you begin mining, there are environmental laws to check out. They are likely to make it more difficult to mine your claim.

One more thing! Before you leave to stake your claim, make sure you can find it again. Putting a post in the ground or piling rocks together is the usual way. And watch out for claim jumpers!

# Where in the World?

Earth is a treasure trove of minerals. Throughout the world, people in different countries are busily mining those minerals. China, for example, is a large producer of tungsten. Tungsten has many electrical uses and is used in alloys; that is, it's fused together with other metals. Tungsten steel is a steel alloy noted for its strength and hardness.

Australia mines iron, aluminum, gold, uranium, and lead. Zaire, a country in Africa, is a leader in mining cobalt. Mexico leads the world in the production of silver ore. South Africa is known as the home of productive gold and diamond mines. South Africa also mines chromium, platinum, and vanadium. Vanadium is another metal used in steel alloys. It increases steel's tensile strength (its ability to stretch) and its resistance to shock.

Closer to home, all 50 of the United States are involved in some kind of mining. The U.S. mining industry is based mostly on digging up construction materials. Sand, gravel, and stone are the largest products, both in volume and value, of our mining companies. Metal ores are also mined in the United States. These include gold, iron, lead, silver, and copper. Arizona leads the country in the value of minerals it excavates. Do you know what is being mined in your state?

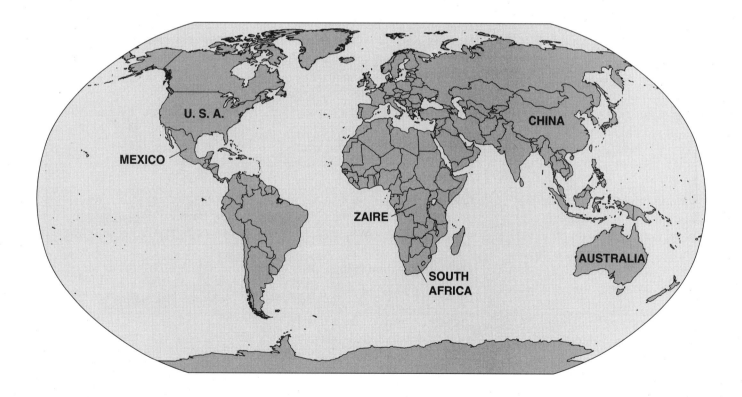

# Mining Production/ Operations Manager

**DAVID RIDINGER
FORMER MINING
PRODUCTION/OPERATIONS
MANAGER
MAGMA COPPER COMPANY
SAN MANUEL, ARIZONA**

In your lifetime, you are likely to use 1,500 pounds of copper. Two-thirds of the nation's copper is produced by four major copper-mining companies in Arizona. I used to be a mining production and operations manager for one of them—the Magma Copper Company. I am now the president of the Arizona Mining Association. We provide information on mining to teachers and the public.

I went to a very small high school where only six of us were interested in math. We were given special advanced math classes. After I graduated, I went to the South Dakota School of Mines. I earned my degree in mining engineering there. My first job was as an underground supervisor and foreman in a copper mine in Chile, a country in South America.

At a copper mine, every day is different. I spend most of my day supervising people and solving problems. Some of the problems are technical. For example, if a cable breaks on one of the shovels, I have to get an electrician to make the repair. I also work with the engineers to inspect the mine and decide whether we are mining in the best places.

Many of the problems I deal with are people problems. For example, when people do not show up for work, I decide what to do. Should I shut down part of the mining operation or find someone in another part of the mine to do the work? I look at my priorities and make a decision.

Automation has changed the mining industry. When I started in the 1950s, there were quite a few underground mines. But they were very expensive and required many workers. Most of the work was done by hand. It took twice as long to extract copper underground as it did on the surface. Thirty years ago, we entered the open-pit era. New machines made it cheaper to mine from above ground, and this made lower-grade deposits economical to mine.

Although there are now more than 60,000 copper-related jobs in the United States, the number of jobs is declining. In 1981, the Arizona copper industry produced 1.2 million tons of new copper with 25,000 workers. In recent years, they produced slightly more tonnage per year with only 12,000 people.

We have bigger trucks and shovels now, too. Trucks once carried 80 tons to 100 tons; now they carry 240 tons. Instead of using 20- to 23-cubic-yard shovels, we now use 40-cubic-yard shovels. One of these big shovels can keep three or four trucks going if it does not break down.

The technology has also changed. A pit mine with five shovels and 20 to 30 trucks can cause a traffic jam. We control traffic by keeping information on computer. Marked trucks pass by a special sensor at the top of the pit. The signal is monitored by a computer. Without the computer, we might have two trucks waiting for loads in one area, and one shovel waiting for a truck in another. With a computer we need fewer trucks.

Mining companies generally recruit and train workers who live in isolated areas near the mines. We like to hire people with at least a high-school education who can think and solve problems. Both women and men drive the big 240-ton trucks, which are automated and air-conditioned.

When you decide to open an abandoned mine, there are a few things to consider. Is the mine on federal land? Chances are it is. It might also be in a designated wilderness area. Starting new mining in these areas is now restricted. If your mine is on federal land, you'll need to file a mining claim under the 1872 mining law.

Next, consider the environmental implications. What does the mine look like? What are those horrible piles? Are you assuming liability for cleanup if you reopen the mine? If a site is contaminated, the federal government will require that you clean it up before you can operate a mine.

You may want to consider open-pit mining. It has a number of advantages. For instance, you do not have to provide underground life support for your workers. But you seldom find minerals, such as copper, on the surface. The copper is likely to be covered with an *overburden*: several hundred feet of soil and rock. You have to lay back the overburden, make waste piles, and dig the hole deep enough to get to the copper. There is no pretty way to do this.

To reduce the environmental impact after the copper has been removed, you can place vegetation on the waste dumps. With copper mining, you are not required to return the land to its original condition. To do so would mean digging another hole to have the material to fill the pits. Although reclaimed mining property will never look the way it did originally, you should try to improve the land and follow all legal requirements.

Now, consider the technical questions in selecting a copper mine. The mining engineer will decide whether the mineral deposits are ample. A 1 percent or more copper content is good. Even if the mineral deposits are plentiful, how much will it cost to mine and process the copper? If you have a small quantity, you do not want to build a smelter on site. A smelter separates impurities from the copper or other pure metals. Small amounts will be shipped to an existing smelter. Is there a smelter nearby?

Economic questions are equally important. In Arizona, the mining industry spends $5.6 billion annually. That is a fairly large contribution to the Arizona economy. But factors that influence the value of copper can change. If the cost of copper is $1.30 today, what will the price be next year? If you operate a mine at a certain rate and have a 10-year copper supply, what might the price of the copper be in 10 years? Who knows? Forecasting copper prices is like throwing a dart at a dart board.

Many factors can influence copper prices. A copper discovery in another country may flood the U.S. market. Power costs could go up. Or you might have metallurgical problems and be unable to extract as much of the copper as you expected. If your workers belong to a union, production costs might be higher. In the past eight years, the price of copper has varied from $0.62 per pound to $1.50 per pound. It's best, of course, to mine more copper when prices increase.

Finally, consider the social issues. Where is the mine located? If it is 50 miles or more outside a city, where will you find workers? Where will they live? Are the people who live near the site willing to have an active mine as a neighbor? Will they oppose it? Also keep in mind that the very high investment in equipment requires managers to operate their mines 24 hours per day, usually seven days per week, and through most holidays.

**Kennecott Corporation's Bingham Canyon Mine is one of the lowest-cost producers in the world.**

# Broken Silence

An important question still remained at Sutter's mill: how much gold awaited discovery? Sutter rode his mule to the sawmill days later. The mill workers were anxious to please the owner with their gold find. They had scattered gold particles in the millrace, the trail of water diverted into the mill. By sprinkling the mill area with gold, the workers thought Sutter could find gold himself.

But of more concern to Sutter was avoiding a real gold rush to his land. In fact, Sutter knew that the potentially gold-rich land surrounding the mill was public land. More to the point, the U.S. Army of President James Polk had defeated Mexico a little more than a week after the Sutter's mill gold find. The peace treaty called for the United States to pay Mexico $15 million for large tracts of land. The deal included land in what would become the states of Nevada, New Mexico, California, and Utah.

Sutter made deals with local Native Americans to obtain the mill land and surrounding area. In exchange for food and clothing, Sutter was able to negotiate a three-year lease for the mill site. He also got nearly a dozen square miles around the sawmill as part of the deal.

Secrets are hard to keep. Word began to leak out about the gold find at Sutter's mill. Mill employees bragged about the gold strike to anyone who would listen. One worker near the mill reportedly galloped into San Francisco on his horse, wildly swinging over his head a bottle full of gold nuggets. "Gold! Gold on the American River!" he shouted.

Just as Sutter had feared, the rush was on. Word spread about the mill site. Many workers deserted Sutter's Fort—which Sutter also called New Helvetia—and headed for the fields of gold.

On March 15, 1848, the *Californian* broke the story with the headline "Gold Mine Found." The article was not front-page news. The small article was put on page 17.

The news spread. As one observer noted at the time, "The farmers have thrown aside their plows, the lawyers their briefs, the doctors their pills, the priests their prayer books . . . and all are now digging gold." Many California towns emptied out as people headed for the promised land of gold and fortune. Even adventurers from as far away as South America, Europe, China, and Australia set out for California.

By mid-July, more than 3,000 miners had made their way to the area. Canvas tents, quickly made shelters, even makeshift stores dotted the hills along the American River. Reports of gold findings in other gullies, streams, sandbars, and ravines spread as fast as the gold was collected. Even President James Polk talked about the gold discovery in his message to Congress in December 1848. The abundance of gold in the territory is of "extraordinary character as would scarcely command belief," Polk reported to Congress. One year after the United States had purchased California, enough gold had been mined in the region to have bought the state three times over.

Some called it a thirst for adventure. Others called it madness. Writer-philosopher Henry David Thoreau considered it simple-minded greed. Whatever the case, thousands sold their possessions to travel to the golden land.

It was official. The California Gold Rush was on!

# CALIFORNIAN.

SAN FRANCISCO, WEDNESDAY MARCH 15, 1849

GOLD MINE FOUND.---In the newly made raceway of the Saw Mill recently erected by Captain Sutter, on the American Fork, gold has been found in considerable quantities. One person brought thirty dollars worth to New Helvetia, gathered there in a short time. California, no doubt, is rich in mineral wealth; great chances here for scientific capitalists. Gold has been found in almost every part of the country.

CALIFORNIAN, MARCH 15, 1849

WEDNESDAY MORNING, DECEMBER 6

### The Gold Fever.

The California gold fever is approaching its crisis. We are told that the new region that has just become a part of our possessions, is El Dorado after all.-- Thither is now setting a tide that will not cease its flow until either-untold wealth is amassed, or extended beggary is secured. By a sudden and accidental discovery, the ground is represented to be one vast gold mine.--Gold is picked up in pure lumps, twenty-four carats fine. Soldiers are deserting their ranks, sailors their ships, and every body their employment, to speed to the region of the gold mines. In a moment, as it were, a desert country, that never deserved much notice from the world, has become the centre of universal attraction. Everybody, by the accounts, is getting money at a rate that puts all past experience in that line far in the shade. The stories are evidently thickening in interest, as do the arithmetical calculations connected with them in importance. Fifteen millions have already come into the possession of *somebody*, and all creation is going out there to fill their pockets with the great condiment of their diseased minds.

HARTFORD COURANT, DECEMBER 6, 1848

The Hartford *Courant* article was printed the day after President Polk's 1848 message to Congess.

# Mine Your Own Business

## Purpose
To design procedures for separating and quantifying and to describe the properties of components in a sample mixture.

## Background
You are a laboratory technician for the Mining Technologies Company (MTC). Your MTC boss has asked you and several other technicians to examine samples collected by field geologists from different areas of a company mine. The mine was closed 50 years when it was no longer making a profit for the company. Efficient new mining techniques may make it profitable to open the mine again.

You have been asked to develop a procedure for extracting minerals from the samples and to determine whether reopening the mine would be profitable. If at least 5 percent of the mineral is usable, the company will make a profit.

The sample tested must be large enough to ensure accuracy. Your results will added to the results of other laboratory technicians investigating samples from different parts of the same mine. The final decision on reopening the mine should be based on data from all the technicians.

## Materials

**For each group:**

- Two 100-ml samples of mixture (from the teacher)
- Screen or piece of wire mesh to act as a sieve
- 100-ml graduated cylinder

- Triple-beam balance
- Small plastic bag
- Sheet of paper
- 500-ml beaker
- Balance      • Water
- Magnet       • Filter paper
- Funnel       • Shallow pan
- Hot plate     • Graph paper

## Procedure
Before you begin, find out from your teacher which materials are the target ores for extraction. Speculate with your partners about how you will use each piece of equipment to separate the components of the mixture.

1. Work with your partners to design a procedure for extracting minerals from your sample. Examine the sample and estimate the percentage of target ores you will extract from the sample.
2. Create a data table to record the information you think you will need when you select the best extraction technique.

3. Weigh each sample. Estimate how many grams of each target ore you might obtain. Work with one sample at a time.
4. Begin your extraction and be very careful to throw nothing away (including the water). Record the properties of all materials as they are separated. This information may be very important later.
5. Once you are finished with the first sample, check your estimate. Was it close to the results you obtained?
6. Before you begin extraction on your second sample, review your first set of extraction procedures. If you change anything, make sure your teacher checks it before you begin.

## Conclusion
Other lab technicians have been examining samples from the same mine. Before making your recommendation on reopening the mine, pool your data for analysis.

1. Use a stem-and-leaf diagram to show the distribution of masses of each mineral recovered by the groups. Use a box-and-whiskers plot to analyze each mineral. How did your results compare with the pooled results? Use the median from each box-and-whiskers plot to make a pie graph showing the percentage (by weight) of each mineral present in the mine.
2. Construct a table for the Environmental Protection Agency (EPA) that shows the

percentages of all products from the mine.

3. As you need at least a 5 percent yield of the target ores, do you think it will be profitable for your company to reopen the mine? Why or why not? Write your recommendation in the form of a memo. Address it to the president of MTC. (Use your teacher's name.) Include data to support your recommendation.

4. After the minerals have been extracted, you must deal with waste products. EPA rules do not allow toxic solid or liquid material to be left at a mine site. It must be either used or reclaimed in some way. Solids that are not toxic can be left on site as long as the landscape is not harmed. The area must be reworked so that you leave it in the same or better condition than it was when you started your mining operation. Write a responsible, step-by-step cleanup procedure for the EPA office in your state.

# Cradles and Sluice Boxes

In the early days of the California Gold Rush, prospectors and miners were in a frenzy. They were willing to try almost anything to find gold and collect it. By 1849, many different methods of gold extraction were being used by these forty-niners.

The wash pan was a simple and popular gold-mining tool. Panning required miners to squat in running water, fill the pan with sediment and gravel, and swirl the pan under the water. They sloshed some of the water over the sides of the pan, washing out the lighter sand and silt and leaving the denser, gold-laden sediments in the pan.

Cradles, long toms, and sluice boxes were "high tech" versions of the wash pan. Workers shoveled sediment into these contraptions and allowed water to run over the sediment. Heavy, gold-bearing sediment was caught behind bars called *riffles.*

Lode gold is the target of hard-rock prospectors. Lode gold is commonly found with quartz, its ore in veins sandwiched between rock layers. It is difficult to separate gold from its surrounding rock when it is found as an ore. An ore is rock with a target metal or mineral in a concentration large enough that it can be mined at a profit.

Early miners sometimes used mercury to separate gold from crushed ore. Mercury would stick to the very fine particles of gold, but it could be easily separated later.

Modern technology has drastically changed mining. Some abandoned gold mines can now be reworked at a profit. Many low-grade ore deposits that were once not economical to mine can now be processed with surprisingly high yields. For example, potassium cyanide leaching is used to separate gold flakes from sand and gravel previously discarded as unusable. After the ore is crushed into a fine powder, a weak

**Man with shovel at a sluice box.**
PHOTO FROM THE CALIFORNIA DEPARTMENT OF PARKS AND RECREATION.

cyanide solution is mixed with it. The resulting mixture, called a slurry, will have small rock particles suspended in it and gold dissolved in it. Filtering removes the fine rock particles. Gold is removed by precipitation on zinc dust or absorption on carbon.

# The Rock Cycle

There are three kinds of rocks on Earth: *igneous, sedimentary,* and *metamorphic.*

Igneous rocks are rocks that have melted or remelted since the formation of Earth's crust about 4 billion years ago. (No rocks remain from that early crust. If they did, they would be igneous, too.)

Sedimentary rock forms when sediments worn from other rocks are deposited and consolidated (combined) into new rock.

Igneous or sedimentary rock can change into metamorphic rock through heat or pressure over a period of time. Right below your feet, our planet is alive with internal and external forces. These forces cause the rock cycle, an ongoing process that builds, destroys, and rebuilds the rocks that form Earth's crust. As you might imagine, this is a very time-consuming process.

Below Earth's crust lies the mantle. Although the mantle is solid, powerful forces deep under Earth's surface cause the mantle to flow. Slow-moving currents of flowing rock actually rise toward the crust and spread out within the mantle. The moving upper mantle carries the crust, which is broken in pieces called *tectonic plates,* on its surface.

On the earth's surface, the main external forces are ones you experience every day— forces related to weather.

Weathering by rain, wind, snow, or glaciers wears down exposed rocks of all kinds. Rivers carry the rock debris to lakes and oceans, where they collect as sediment. Some sediments become consolidated into sedimentary rock.

Slowly colliding tectonic plates thrust much of this sedimentary rock above the sea, forming islands, mountains, and other landforms. (This sedimentary rock, now exposed to the forces of weathering, can be worn down again to become a new generation of sedimentary rock.) Plates undergoing subduction— the process where one plate moves under another plate— carry igneous and sedimentary rock down into the mantle. Here heat and pressure transform the igneous and sedimentary rock into metamorphic rock.

Molten igneous rock rises through the cooler, denser rocks surrounding volcanoes. The volcanic activity creates island arcs such as Alaska's Aleutian Islands. It also injects new material into the crust and bakes preexisting rocks.

Igneous rocks contain many minerals, primarily silicates. Silicates are compounds formed from silicon, oxygen, and various metals. The most common metals that form silicates are aluminum, iron, magnesium, calcium, sodium, and potassium. Silicon is found in quartz and opal. Silicon is the second most abundant element on earth after oxygen.

The most abundant silicates are called *feldspars.* Granite— made of quartz, feldspar, and mica—is the chief igneous rock in the continental crust.

The type of rock formed depends on the original type of

## The Rock Cycle

magma and its cooling history. Different minerals crystallize, or "freeze out," and separate at different temperatures. The rate of cooling determines the size of the crystals. Slow cooling produces large mineral crystals; fast cooling generates fine-grained rocks.

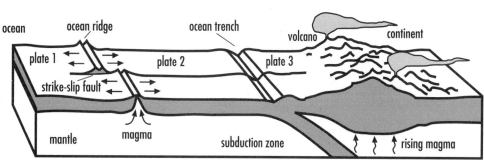

## Mantle forces and plates

*Cross section of plate boundaries formed by ocean ridges (rift zones), strike-slip faults, and subduction zones.*

DISCOVERY FILE

# Sedimentary Rock

More than three-quarters of the earth's crust is covered by a skin of sediments. The skin has formed gradually. Erosion of mountains and soil produces debris that settles on the beds of lakes and rivers. Animals and plants live and die in the upper layers of the oceans. Their remains settle to the ocean floor, adding to the sediments collecting there. Over the years, the layer of sediments grows deeper and deeper.

The weight of new sediments being added from above squeezes water from the deeper sediments. The deepest particles become tightly packed together, forming sedimentary rock. The process where loose sediment turns to solid rock is called *lithification.* Certain minerals laid down among the sediments help cement the mass together.

Some sedimentary rocks, such as limestone, are made up mostly of plant and animal remains. The bodies of these plants and animals are rich in calcium. When the bodies decay, the calcium remains.

Other sedimentary rocks, called *clastic* rocks, are made from tiny pieces of weathered rock. Sandstone is an example of a clastic rock.

As water moves, it sorts weathered rock fragments according to size and density. Large-grained pieces form sedimentary rock known as *conglomerates;*

medium-sized grains become rocks such as sandstone; and fine-grained particles come together to form clay and then solidify as shale.

The next time you see a deep cut in the earth's crust, remember that the layers you see are sediments deposited long ago.

*The Grand Canyon.* PHOTO BY JOE BRILLA.

# Limestone: What's in It for You?

Limestone does not sparkle as diamonds do. It is not treasured like gold. But limestone is a national necessity, and it holds a wealth of information about Earth's history.

Limestone is rich in fossils. It is the favorite rock of many paleontologists. Its fossils tell much about the evolution of marine life on earth. Limestone also tells about some of the earth's geologic history.

Some of the plants and animals preserved as fossils in limestone were neighbors of dinosaurs. Others lived, died, and were preserved long before dinosaurs left their footprints. Even dinosaur footprints are considered fossils.

Limestone is a sedimentary rock usually formed by the remains of plants and animals deposited on the sea floor.

So why is there a limestone quarry in Winston-Salem, North Carolina, more than 300 kilometers (185 miles) from the ocean? One explanation is that the sea level was once much higher than it is now. Can you think of other possible reasons?

You will find limestone used all around you. It is used in buildings and roads. It is used to purify the water that comes out your tap and the wastewater that flows down your drains.

As part of the Task, your team is asked to predict the future. You must speculate on the value of gold, silver, copper, diamond, and limestone in the years to come.

As you wonder about the future, consider this: The U.S. government will never buy you a diamond ring or a gold watch. But even when times are tough, governments and industries will provide limestone. Limestone will always be useful for buildings and roads.

Limestone does not sell for as much as diamonds and gold do, but it does not cost as much to mine, either. Quarries are on or near the surface. Gold and diamond mines usually go deep below the earth's surface, and digging deep is expensive.

# As Good as Gold

The gold standard is a worldwide monetary system. A country using the gold standard will exchange its paper money for a fixed quantity of gold.

In the early 1900s, the United States used a gold standard. In fact, at the end of World War I, the United States would convert paper money into gold coins. That is where the saying about paper money being "as good as gold" comes from.

During World War II, however, America abandoned the gold standard. The country adopted a modified gold standard after World War II.

Some nations of the world today still use gold in their monetary transactions. The United States has huge guarded vaults containing a large part of its gold stocks. The gold is kept in the form of bullion or bars. These vaults are located in the Fort Knox Bullion Depository. The depository is 30 miles southwest of Louisville, Kentucky.

Paper money and coins—often represented by checks and credit cards—rather than gold are widely used today in most countries as a primary means of payment.

# Field Geologist

JOE GUTIERREZ
FIELD GEOLOGIST (RETIRED)
VULCAN MATERIALS
COMPANY, LIMESTONE
QUARRY
WINSTON-SALEM, NORTH
CAROLINA

For 35 years, I have worked at Vulcan Materials in North Carolina. I am a field geologist. Limestone quarries are my specialty. Vulcan Materials manages 129 quarries—the largest limestone quarry operation in the U. S.

A quarry is an open pit where stone, slate, or limestone are mined. We provide crushed stone to contractors who use it to make concrete and asphalt for buildings and roads. We also sell limestone products to water-purification and sewage plants.

I am retired from full-time work at Vulcan. Now I am a consultant for them. Because I know the geology of our quarries, they call me for help.

Sometimes I work at the museum named after me, speaking to students and teachers about geology, mining, and fossils.

Limestone is made of fossils. We often find brachiopods, trilobites, and other fossils. The museum has about 100 rock specimens and mineral displays.

The museum also is a core storage facility. We have core samples from when I started working there in 1959. We use the cores as a reference. Rather than going back and redrilling a site, we pull an old sample. Then

we run tests to see whether it meets current needs.

Workdays can be very long for field geologists. We often work from 7:00 a.m. to 7:00 p.m. during the summer. We work as late as daylight permits during the winter.

I grew up in the city, but I was always interested in rocks and exploring. In college, I took math, physics, and chemistry. Today, a geologist also needs to know calculus and have good writing skills.

When I started in field geology, the interstate highway system was just being built. They needed crushed stone for asphalt and cement. My first job was locating the quarry sites.

Hauling stone is expensive. It was cheaper to open a quarry nearby than to haul the stone long distances, so we tried to put a quarry site in the middle of every job. We situated a quarry about every 14 miles.

We first had to locate a site and lease the property. Next, we drilled through the *overburden*, or soil, to determine how far below we would find rock. We drilled core samples, logged their locations, and tested them.

State and federal highway boards required tests to check how well the rock would withstand traffic. We conducted about ten tests on each core sample. We had our own laboratory where we tested strength, hardness, and freezing characteristics.

Today, finding a site for a quarry can be hard. Most abandoned quarries have not run out of rock. Population and other factors determine which quarries stay open. If a quarry is too close to where people live, they complain. But if the stone has to be shipped from other places, it costs 13–20¢ per mile. This adds tremendously to the cost.

What is the demand for limestone? There has to be a market large enough to support a renewed operation. How much is left in the old quarry? Quarries cannot be opened unless they have at least 40 years of reserve. A 40-year reserve allows a company to make a profit.

To make sure the reserves you need are there, drill cores around the old quarry. You may need to use seismology techniques to check the types of rock.

Test blasts are also used to determine what impact blasting might have on people living in the area. You do not want the ground to shake enough to rattle dishes or cause cracks in the walls of nearby houses.

▶ continued from page 25

Because of environmental and zoning laws, you cannot place quarries just anywhere. People are concerned about groundwater and air pollution. They also do not want plant and animal life destroyed. Plans for water use, dust control, noise and air pollution must be submitted.

Laws require quarries to be more than 250 feet from a main highway. They also require that the location of every piece of equipment be approved. It can take about two years and between $200,000 and $500,000 to obtain the needed zoning.

When we finally get permission, we lease more land than we will actually use. The extra land acts as a buffer zone. We build a *berm,* or mound, in the buffer zone. We make it about 20 feet high. Then we plant vegetation on the slopes and trees on top. The berm and trees screen the quarry from sight. They also help contain the dust and reduce noise.

Another problem is asbestos. Breathing asbestos dust can cause lung cancer, so every mineral at the site has to be tested for purity.

We scan each mineral with an electron microscope. We must be sure asbestos is not present.

The intended use of the mineral helps determine which abandoned quarry to reopen. Sulfide causes cracks in concrete. If we find sulfide in rocks, we cannot use those rocks to build highways. Sulfide also causes concrete blocks to fade.

Did you know that limestone is used in chewing gum? It is also used in making glue, paper, soap, and medicine. You would be surprised at how many products in our lives come from rocks.

# Lightweight Aggregate

Aggregate is a composite, or mixture, of different materials. Vulcan Materials produces lightweight aggregate. They use heat to expand shale and slate to three times their normal volume. Workers building high-rise buildings can pump slurries made from this lightweight aggregate about three and a half times higher than they can pump slurries made from unexpanded rock.

Lightweight aggregate is also used for insulating. Insulation keeps buildings warm in the winter and cool in the summer.

Lightweight aggregate is also used to make bridges and roads lighter, yet it is strong enough to carry the weight of automobiles. It makes structures more flexible than heavy cement can. It is a good building material for earthquake-prone areas.

# Seismology in Construction

If you were planning to build a highway, you would need to know about the rocks beneath the location of the road. But you cannot drill core samples every foot of the way. You could, however, use seismology.

Seismology is the study of how vibrations pass through the ground. Vibrations behave differently based on the kind of material they pass through.

Fifty years ago, geologists beat a 10-pound hammer on the ground. They used instruments to listen to the vibrations some distance away. Later, geologists shot 12-gauge shotgun shells into the ground. The blast provided more energy to measure. Nowadays, one-third of a stick of dynamite and a blasting cap set off even stronger underground waves. Geologists measure these waves with sensitive instruments.

The construction industry has pioneered these and other ways to identify underground rock formations. Each technique tells a slightly different story about the unseen rock layers below. As the energy has increased, so has the detail in the picture being drawn.

# The Forty-Niners

They called themselves the forty-niners because the Gold Rush started in 1849. Two important tools sustained their quest—a shovel and a pan. The pan proved valuable for other duties besides searching for gold. Miners could also wash their clothes, feed their mules, and even cook in a tin or iron pan.

Panning in cold rivers meant long hours of swishing gravel-and-sand-laden water around and around. Gold, being a denser material, would sink to the bottom of the pan. The sand and gravel, less dense and lighter in weight, would fall over the edge of the pan.

Gold mining was a numbing experience for many miners. A miner might find a few particles of gold in the pan—eventually. A miner often spent the entire day squatting near a stream to sift through 50 pans of dirt and gravel.

Once separated from the mud, sand, and gravel, gold might be found in one of three forms: dust, flakes, or nuggets. For a gold miner in 1849, the established worth of one troy ounce of gold was $20.67. Many early arrivals to California did well. At times, a day of panning yielded nearly $3,000 worth of gold. One lucky team of miners cleared $50,000 in a day's work. Such reports helped fuel Gold-Rush fever to new levels. But for most miners, $10 to $20 worth of gold a day was typical. And rising costs of food and supplies would eat away most of that amount.

Staking a claim was easy. All a miner had to do was pick a spot, drive wooden stakes to mark the claim, and tack up a sign. Then the tough work could begin. The lucky prospector who actually struck pay dirt had to keep a wary eye open for claim jumpers.

By far the most common experience was hard work with little reward. Back-breaking efforts of digging into rock and coming up with an ounce a day was standard. After expenses, a typical prospector was left with $5 or $6 profit each day. That's not bad considering a job as a common laborer only paid half that much. Still, the gold and the riches it could bring to a lucky miner were a lure to many.

There were tricks to the gold-mining trade. Spotting a good location for gold prospecting required some knowledge of basic geology and mineralogy. Reddish dirt proved more rewarding than other surface colors. However, nature sometimes played its own tricks. Many a miner was misled by fool's gold. It took more than a careful eye to sort out real gold from fake gold. Iron pyrite—fool's gold—shatters under pressure and is gritty between the teeth. Gold can be mashed flat and feels smooth to the teeth.

Many successful gold miners brought their nuggets and gold dust to the U.S. Mint in San Francisco. There, the gold would be weighed. The Mint had to shut down its offices on occasion just to clean up all the gold dust. Every two years, officials had to tear up the mint's carpets and burn them. From the ashes, enough gold was recovered to buy new carpets—with money left over.

California was being transformed. Whether for better or for worse has yet to be determined.

**STUDENT VOICES**

I liked gold panning. It was fun. But I didn't like not being able to pick the gold up when I found it. It was too small.

**JAMES LIANG**
**NORTH POTOMAC, MD**

# Getting to the Core of the Matter

## Purpose

To investigate rock layers using core-sampling techniques.

## Background

A group of investors is interested in buying stock in your company. They know it will be two or three years before you begin to show a profit, but they might be willing to invest now. All you have to do is convince them that the mine your company might reopen has an adequate supply of mineral. They have seen the test results on the abandoned sections of the mine. Now they want to see nine core samples taken from the surrounding area. Core sampling will show the location of additional ore and how much is available.

The investors do not want you to recommend whether to buy the stock. They just want the data displayed in the form of a three-dimensional graph.

## Materials

**For each pair:**

- 1 geological model of the area (cupcake or clay)
- 6 clear plastic straws
- Metric ruler
- 2 sheets of two-sided graph paper
- Clear tape
- Colored pencils or markers
- Scissors

## Procedure

1. To make a three-dimensional graph of the area, fold two sheets of graph paper and arrange them as shown in Figure A.
   a. Fold one sheet of graph paper in half on one of its vertical grid lines. Fold a second sheet of graph paper the same way.
   b. Put the two folded edges together so they touch with the unfolded, long edges outward. All horizontal lines on front, back, and sides of the graph must line up.
   c. Tape the two sheets together along the folded edge.
   d. Label the *x*, *y*, and *z* axes.
   e. Open the graph so you have an X-shaped figure when looking down from one edge.

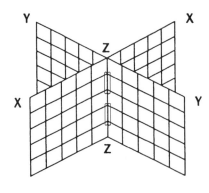

**Figure A**
**Three-Dimensional Grid**
**Each angle *xyz* is a folded sheet of graph paper taped along *z*.**

2. Measure the depth of your model; then select an appropriate scale for your graph. A good scale is one that uses most of the graph. You may exaggerate the depth or width measurement.

3. Construct a data table for keeping track of the thickness of each layer for nine core samples.

4. Figure B shows the places to take the nine core samples in your model as if you are looking down on the model. Push a clear plastic straw through the model at one of the sites. Pull the straw out and cut it just above the core sample. The different colors in your core sample represent different rock layers.

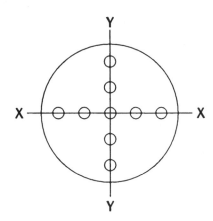

**Figure B**
**Plot core samples on the z axis.**

5. Plot your core samples on the three-dimensional graph. Color your graph with the colors that correspond to the rock layers in the model. Show the rock layers on all sides of the graph, using the colors you have selected.

6. Prepare a legend for your graph.

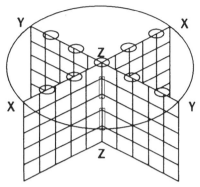

**Figure C**
*This shows how the core samples relate to the graph.*

## Conclusion

1.  Once you have removed core samples and completed the three-dimensional graph, decide where to drill the mine shaft. It is easier to drill through sedimentary rock than metamorphic or igneous rock.
2.  Your teacher will post a key showing which colors represent which rock layers in your model. Analyze your core samples using the key, and then decide where to drill your mine shaft.
3.  Write a letter to the investors. Explain why you decided to place the mine shaft where you did.

# Mining Law

In 1872, the U.S. Congress passed the General Mining Law. This mining law was written to promote economic development in the western United States. The legislation allowed explorers to prospect, stake a claim, and mine on federal lands. Federal lands are owned by the U.S. government.

Many prospectors took advantage of the General Mining Law. Metallic minerals, such as gold, silver, copper, lead, and zinc have all been mined from federal lands.

Originally, the law allowed miners access to federal land on a first-come, first-served basis. Prospectors could stake a claim without first asking permission from the federal government. Prospectors didn't pay the government for use of the land, even if they struck it rich.

For nearly 125 years, the General Mining Law of 1872 has been in effect. However, there have been some changes in how the General Mining Law is enforced. Today, large amounts of federal land are off limits. Mining companies are no longer allowed to start new mining operations in designated wilderness areas. If a company is already mining an area that is later designated as a wilderness area, it can continue mining.

Federal lands containing oil, gas, or coal are now leased to companies. These companies pay royalties to the government for use of this land. Federal lands containing nonmetallic minerals such as phosphorus and potash are also leased.

Another important change to the mining law involves the environment. Mineral exploration on federal lands now requires a variety of permits. These permits force a close look at the environmental consequences of exploring and mining federal lands.

More and more, federal lands are being eyed for recreation use. Today, mining must compete with these and other land uses. Environmental protection of these lands versus the need to mine is a hotly debated topic. The General Mining Law of 1872 may be reformed in the next few years.

# 'Great terrain robbery': Up to $10 billion in gold

By Linda Kanamine
USA TODAY

WASHINGTON — "The biggest gold heist since the days of Butch Cassidy" — a bargain sale of 1,793 acres of gold-rich federal land — was reluctantly approved Monday by Interior Secretary Bruce Babbitt.

Canada-based Barrick Goldstrike Mines Inc. now owns the sagebrush-covered hills in Carlin, Nev., and an estimated $10 billion in gold below. Cost: $5 an acre or $8,965.

"These are public assets basically being given away," Babbitt says. "It's a ripoff."

It's also the law.

The 1872 Mining Act, passed to encourage Western settlers, gives those who stake a valid claim on public land cheap access to minerals, without having to pay royalties.

Even today, mining companies can file patents to buy that land for $2.50 to $5 an acre.

"That barren rock in a desolate desert didn't have any value until Barrick came along, started exploring, took the risk and invested $1 billion" to mine there, says Barrick vice president Vince Borg.

But Babbitt — standing by a giant blue bank check made out to Barrick for $10 billion and signed "The American People" — used the day to push for mining law reform.

Senate and House conferees will have to work out big differences in their bills.

Babbitt says he wants royalties, greater environmental protection and an end to the federal land giveaways.

More than 500 other patent applications are pending with the Bureau of Land Management and Forest Service.

Says Sierra Club's Kathryn Hohmann: "This is the great terrain robbery."

USA TODAY, MAY 17, 1994

**ENDANGERED:** Independent prospectors Ardith and William Anell.

## Change 1872 mining law before it's too late to stop taxpayer rip-off by giant corporations

USA TODAY's story of the gold mining rip-off was just the tip of the iceberg (" 'Great terrain robbery': Up to $10 billion in gold," News).

If the American people do not demand their representatives change the 1872 Mining Act now, get ready to report on an additional $83 billion worth of gold, silver and other minerals that will be ripped off in the next few years. That's how much publicly owned gold and other minerals are about to be sold to mining companies for a pittance.

As independent prospectors, we are two of the remaining few who helped build the U.S. mining industry. We discovered three Nevada mines — one world-class — with combined production of more than 1.5 million ounces of gold and 35 million ounces of silver.

About all that's left of hard-rock mining in the USA is conducted by huge national and multinational corporations, using giant earthmoving equipment. They can acquire huge claims of hundreds of square miles, patent mineralized claims, mine vast amounts of ore and reap large profits under the law expressly written for small-scale prospectors and miners.

To continue letting giant companies operate under the 1872 law tilts the playing field and compels independent prospectors to abandon their chosen work. It also causes other problems:

▶ Large-scale methods are incompatible with the environment, using vast amounts of non-renewable resources to extract minute amounts of gold and silver.

▶ Patenting mining claims turns public land over to private ownership.

▶ Fast depletion of ore deposits by giant earthmovers means short-term jobs for a few people. Then comes unemployment, environmental disaster and disappointment for future generations.

U.S. citizens do not share in the profits but are expected to pay for environmental mistakes not of their making and to casually allow natural resources to be removed for the benefit of a few corporations, many of which are foreign-owned and whose home governments will not allow U.S. citizens to prospect or mine in their countries.

Why shouldn't the U.S. taxpayer get a fair return? The longer we hold onto the antiquated law, the faster we lose claim to our natural resources, and the faster independent miners, and the public, lose faith in their government.

William and Ardith Anell
Cedarville, Calif.

USA TODAY, JULY 22, 1994

# Mining law robs taxpayers

**While Congress delays reform, an 1872 law lets miners plunder public land, costing the U.S. millions.**

A gold rush is under way that needs to be stopped quickly.

At least 27 companies are rushing to buy government land at 19th century prices — $2.50 to $5 an acre — on which they have been mining metals, mostly gold, for years.

They're rushing because Congress is threatening to change the 1872 law that allows anyone to file a claim and freely mine the vast Western acreages owned by the taxpayers and controlled by the U.S. Bureau of Land Management.

A House-passed bill would charge royalties on metals taken from federal land and impose tough environmental and land-restoration regulations where no rules now exist. But as Congress bickers and dickers, mining companies are using the 1872 law to beat the changes.

They can buy the land they've claimed, at prices fixed 122 years ago, and be out from under any new rules. If the miners meet a few simple tests, such as proving the land contains valuable metal, the government is required to sell. The House bill would repeal this part of the law.

Interior Secretary Bruce Babbitt called it a "gold heist" in May when he signed papers selling the 1,949-acre Goldstrike mines near Elko, Nev., to American Barrick Resources. Price: $9,675. The mines have 30 million ounces of gold. At Friday's closing price of $385 an ounce, that's worth $11.55 billion.

If the government owned the land, the 8% royalty imposed by the House bill would bring the Treasury $925 million.

While a bloc of Western senators stalls congressional action, holding out for weaker changes, other companies are following the Goldstrike lead:

▶ Noranda Minerals proposes to buy the New World Mine in Montana, three miles from Yellowstone Park, for $220.

▶ Arizona Mining Co. wants the Sanchez Mine in the Coronado National Forest — and its 550,000 tons of copper — for $1,640.

▶ Independence Mining Co. offers $5,080 for Nevada's Jerritt Canyon Mine and gold worth $1.1 billion.

Total price for 27 pending sales: $77,600.

It's a legal rip-off that Congress, if inclined, could end tomorrow. Bills have passed both houses. A compromise between the two is on the table. Every day that House-Senate negotiators waste without settling their differences is another day their constituents' pockets can be picked.

Stop the gold rush. Now.

USA TODAY, JULY 25, 1994.

## 1872 Mining Law yields wealth of benefits

Your editorial, "Mining law robs taxpayers," took a look at mining on public lands through the wrong end of the telescope (Our View, Debate, Monday).

Managed, scientifically sound mining development on federal lands brings a multitude of benefits to the country as a whole, far more than the return on investment that goes to individuals and corporations securing those mining rights.

It is unfair that you used the glittering mineral gold — "mostly gold" is how you put it — to draw attention to the wealth of beneficial metals, chemicals and soils that have been produced over the years via the regulations of the 1872 Mining Law.

Dental X-rays and nuclear medicines that defeat the spread of cancers are just two of the health benefits based upon minerals "mostly" extracted under 1872 Mining Law provisions.

Copper that juices electronics and "rare earths" that give color to videography are among the elements that brighten life because they "mostly" were discovered with the 1872 Mining Law.

Factor in hundreds of thousands, even millions, of jobs and lives affected by the production from lands opened in the past by the 1872 Mining Law, and you have a nation that "mostly" benefits from this wisdom distilled 122 years ago and fine-tuned since.

A complete junking of the law, based upon some subjectively viewed excesses, is micromanagement at its worst and "mostly" doesn't benefit the overwhelming majority of the nation.

Keep the 1872 Mining Law; toss out the bath-water arguments against it.

John Ponce, exec. coordinator
Alta California Alliance
Eureka, Calif.

USA TODAY, JULY 27, 1994.

# Mining the taxpayers

The sickening thud you heard late last week in Congress was the sound of the U.S. Senate dropping billions of dollars in mineral rights at the door of large mining companies — no charge, of course.

A few Western-state senators threatened a filibuster, and — *poof!* — reform of the 1872 Mining Law died. Mining companies can continue buying federal land containing billions of dollars in precious metals for as little as $2.50 an acre, and then extract the minerals free of charge.

Miners get rich. The public gets ripped off. Rep. George Miller, chairman of the House Committee on Natural Resources, says miners have extracted more than $230 billion worth of gold and other minerals over the past 120 years. Taxpayers didn't get a penny.

That deal isn't just fat; it's grotesque. Even the powerful coal, oil and natural gas industries pay a royalty — 12.5%. Yet when Congress started talking about reform, the mining industry howled at the prospect of paying even 8%. A hodgepodge of Western and conservative lawmakers managed to dicker the price down to a scandalously low 3.5%, and the industry *still* prevailed on them to scuttle the proposal.

Adding tang to your bile: Foreign corporations own or control more than half of the 40 largest gold mines in the nation. In other words, a handful of senators not only robbed the taxpayers, they did so largely for the benefit of foreign investors.

Defenders of the law say they are saving jobs. And it is true that there's been massive job loss in mining — 80% in the past 20 years. But that's due entirely to modernization initiated by the mining companies. You can't blame federal reformers for that.

Fact is, the 1872 law was designed to encourage westward migration and so is anachronistic on its face.

Moreover, reforming it can only benefit Western states. The new royalties, for example, would have been used to clean up mining-related pollution. This, in turn, would have provided a new and lasting source of jobs for endangered workers and returned tens of millions of dollars to local economies.

What to do? In the short term, the Interior Department can use its authority to limit new mining and new mining claims. But only Congress can stop the rip-off entirely.

Come the new year, voters should demand Congress stop selling the nation's minerals for a lousy $2.50 a throw and start acting like a respectable steward of public resources.

USA TODAY, OCTOBER 4, 1994

# Mining reformers have selves to blame for defeat

USA TODAY's suggestion that mine cleanup jobs can somehow offset the thousands of high-paying mining jobs that would have been lost under mining-law-reform proposals considered by Congress this year was ludicrous ("Mining the taxpayers," Editorial, Tuesday).

Such reclamation jobs are short-term, low-wage, low-skill positions that add no real value to domestic output.

To assert that they are a "lasting source of jobs" that would return "millions of dollars to local economies" was irresponsible and untrue.

To blame modernization for job losses that have occurred in the industry over the past 20 years was nonsense. The regulatory and economic uncertainty created by the debate over mining-law reform has caused many mining companies to look overseas for mineral-development opportunities.

Companies have spent substantially less in U.S. exploration and development activities and, consequently, a cutback in mining-related jobs has occurred.

The past two years, the mining industry has supported reasonable proposals to update the U.S. mining law without throwing thousands of Americans out of work. We agreed to pay a fair royalty for mining on federal lands and to abolish the existing patent system. We abide by nearly two dozen federal environmental laws. Additionally, we are required by states to clean up mining sites and to protect water quality.

Time and again, however, mining critics have rejected responsible proposals in favor of more onerous legislation that would cost thousands of jobs and millions of tax dollars. Anti-mining advocates have no one to blame but themselves for the death of mining reform this year.

Jack Gerard
Mining Resources Alliance
Washington, D.C.

USA TODAY, OCTOBER 7–9, 1994

# Microscopic Miners: Using Biotechnology to Recover Metals

Sometimes it is hard to remove metals from ores. (Ores are rocks containing useful metals.) Leaching is a mining process that passes chemicals through ore to dissolve out valuable metals. But leaching does not always work.

*Biotechnology* researchers at the U.S. Bureau of Mines laboratories are experimenting with a new type of tiny miner. Have they trained fleas to don hard hats and excavate very small deposits? No, but they have found strains of bacteria that actually mine valuable metals. By eating ore-bearing rocks, then concentrating the undigestible metals within their bodies, these little micro-miners are helping researchers recover copper and silver from hard-to-leach ores.

Scientists are also exploring the use of these microscopic miners to remove contaminants from mining wastes. Bacteria, algae, and fungi are proving helpful in removing toxic metals such as cadmium and selenium from the wastewater flowing from mines.

# Harvesting the Ocean

Undersea mining is thought to have started a long time ago. About 2,000 years ago, the Greeks were able to remove lead and zinc ores from under Mediterranean waters.

Today, miners use tunneling to recover rich undersea deposits of coal. Nearly 30 percent of Japan's coal resources comes from underwater mining.

An even greater resource sits right on the ocean floors. Large nodules of copper, iron, nickel, manganese, and cobalt lie on the ocean bottom. It has been estimated that 1.5 trillion tons of these nodules exist in the Pacific Ocean basin alone.

These nodules, or clumps of minerals, were first discovered in the 1800s. Only in recent years has the technology for mining the nodules from depths of 12,000 feet and below become available. Companies haul in both resources and profit by mining these natural ores. Scientists have also explored the practicality of mining inactive underwater volcanoes for precious metals.

For years, disputes between countries have slowed underwater mining. Who owns these resources? Do resources dredged up from the ocean bottom belong to everyone? If so, should the profits made from such mining be shared?

Fearing loss of territory and profits, several coastal countries have extended their national boundaries 200 miles offshore. They call this area between the 12-mile traditional boundary and the new 200-mile boundary their "exclusive economic zone."

Debates over how best to control mining the oceans have gone on for years. These viewpoints have been aired at Law of the Sea conferences held at the United Nations.

# Metallurgical Engineer

JOHN RAJALA
CHIEF METALLURGICAL
ENGINEER, SILVER
HECLA MINING COMPANY
COEUR D'ALENE, IDAHO

I am the chief metallurgical engineer for Hecla Mining Company. My work involves processing ores to extract precious metals such as silver and gold. At most of our mines, we recover gold and silver from the same ore.

For the last few years, I have been designing our new mining project at the Grouse Creek Gold and Silver Mine in central Idaho. Grouse Creek is an old gold-mining district with a lot of old tunnels running under it. The Idaho gold rush really opened up that part of central Idaho.

Working on new projects is what I like best about my job. Workers drill cores and remove ore samples. We *assay*, or examine, the samples, looking for the metals we think are found there.

There are different ways to assay for gold and silver. The most common way is by fire. First, we crush the ore and grind it down to a very fine size. Then, we remove a small sample for the fire-assay procedure. The sample is processed several times to recover the gold and silver.

Once we have the gold and silver, we weigh it and then separate the metals from each other. We use nitric acid to separate silver from gold. We weigh the sample again. The difference in weight tells us how much gold is in the ore.

We develop a flow chart for the recovery of the metals from the ore; then the engineering starts. The engineer designs a processing plant. A working model of the plant and mine is built. The model helps us better understand the project before it is actually built.

After the engineering phase, we build the processing plant and dig tunnels. When that is finished, we start up the mine.

When the ore is processed on a large industrial scale, we use sodium cyanide to separate the gold and silver from the ore. Once the ore is processed at our plant, we ship the concentrate to a smelter. At the smelter the final operation separates the silver from the gold.

There are many uses for silver. The two largest uses are in photography and electronics. Photographic films contain silver compounds that darken when exposed to light. Because silver is an excellent, reliable conductor, it is used in some electronic circuitry. Silver is a better conductor of electricity than copper. But copper is used in most electrical circuits because it's less expensive.

I have bachelor's and master's degrees in metallurgical engineering. In this field, I must use math every day. Many of the processes used to remove metal from ore use mathematical models. For example, in the grinding process, various mathematical equations come close to describing the process. We use mathematical equations to explain most other processes in the recovery of metals.

A good chemistry background is also essential for understanding the way recovery processes work. Most recovery projects use chemical processes. Without knowledge of general chemistry and metallurgical chemistry, it would be difficult to know how a process is working and to improve the process of extracting metal from the ore.

Though a sound mathematics and science background is essential in mining, math and science are also important to every well-rounded person. Computer skills are also becoming more important in mining. Strong oral- and written-communication skills are necessary, too.

If possible, try to take a tour of a mine. There are mines in every state and in many foreign countries.

Today, there are a lot of opportunities for people with mining-related training—especially in the fields of geology, mining engineering, and metallurgical engineering.

# Westward Ho!

Sixteenth-century Spanish explorers called the land in the northwestern part of the New World *California*, after a treasure island in a popular story of the time. After winning its independence from Spain in 1821, Mexico—which included what is now California—was an isolated and ignored province.

In 1848, the California territory was an agricultural frontier settled by a few hundred men and women. One year later, the gold fields lured some 62,000 people hungry with the promise of instant riches.

By land, by sea, and from all over the globe, the forty-niners made their way to California. Ships, schooners, and steamers pulled into the San Francisco port. The small town grew to a city of 25,000 residents. Swarms of miners and would-be miners made their way to California's central valleys and up the western slopes of the Sierra Nevada. Like San Francisco, Sacramento also grew in population. California's rapid growth led to its being granted statehood as a free (not slave) state in 1850. By that time, mining was California's main occupation. Three out of every five inhabitants of the state were miners.

From the eastern United States, tens of thousands of wagons rumbled westward. For many, travel by land was a brutal, unforgiving hardship. The trek was a three- to five-month ordeal. They came across mountains, deserts, and rivers—passing the remains of those who did not survive the journey. Land trails to California were strewn with crude grave markers, burned-out wagons, broken wagon wheels, rotting food, and hundreds of dead animals.

Gold fever brought with it a harsh lifestyle. Fist fights and shootings were common. Drunk and disorderly conduct was the rule of the day. An evening's gambling and drinking could cost a miner what had taken him a week to gather. A nightly brawl or two was commonplace in most mining camps.

The price of tools and other commodities skyrocketed. Items in short supply were sold for many ➤

➤ continued on page 36

THE
# EMIGRANTS' GUIDE
TO
## CALIFORNIA,
CONTAINING EVERY POINT OF INFORMATION FOR THE EMIGRANT-INCLUDING ROUTES, DISTANCES, WATER, GRASS, TIMBER, CROSSING OF RIVERS, PASSES, ALTITUDES, WITH A LARGE MAP OF ROUTES, AND PROFILE OF COUNTRY, &C.,-WITH FULL DIRECTIONS FOR TESTING AND ASSAYING GOLD AND OTHER ORES.

BY JOSEPH E. WARE.

PUBLISHED BY J. HALSALL,
NO. 124 MAIN STREET
ST. LOUIS, MO.

A primer for the overland route

For gold seekers traveling overland, Joseph Ware's 1849 guide served as an invaluable source book. Its title page (above) indicates the range of its contents; examples of its pithy, practical advice appear below.

*Start at 4 – travel till the sun gets high – camp till the heat is over. Then start again and travel till dark.*

*After the upper Platte Ford, for over fifty miles, the water is impregnated with poisonous matter. If you would avoid sickness, abandon its use.*

*TRUCKIE'S PASS. You will be tried to the utmost. Pack everything over the summit, then haul your wagons up with ropes. You will certainly save time, and perhaps hundreds of dollars.*

▶ continued from page 35

times their true worth. Water was very precious for drinking and especially for mining operations distant from streams.

Many who came to California made their fortunes not from the gold itself, but from gold-mining services. John Studebaker migrated from Indiana to Placerville, California. There, Studebaker produced wheelbarrows for miners. In five years, Studebaker saved $8,000. He later returned to Indiana, adding his money to the family fortune. Years later, the family business blossomed into one of America's most successful carriage makers.

A similar story involved Levi Strauss. Sailing from New York in 1850, Strauss arrived in San Francisco with a single bolt of canvas tenting. He transformed the heavy canvas into a pair of pants for a miner. Later, to reinforce seams on his pants design, Strauss used little copper rivets. In just one year, the pants maker was the top producer of the durable pants throughout California. Even today, his pants are known as Levi's.

# House ponders value of mining on public lands

By Linda Kanamine
USA TODAY

The strident struggle over Western land traditions enters another round today when the House begins debate on mining law reform.

Rhetoric and emotions run deep for those hoping to update the 121-year-old law.

"It's a matter of whether the U.S. wants a mining industry or not. It's as simple as that," says Linda Findlay of Phelps-Dodge Corp., a leading copper mining company. "We want to stay in this country. (But) it's a fairly high-stakes game."

Counters Jean Clark of Montana's Northern Plains Resource Council: "It is time for . . . critical watersheds, agricultural production, wildlife habitat and recreational opportunities to be weighed fairly against the value of mining."

When President Grant signed the 1872 Mining Law, it was an attempt to lure people and business to the untamed, unsettled West.

Little has changed in the law: Stake a valid claim and get cheap access to minerals without paying royalties. With proof of a valuable deposit, claim-holders can buy land for $5 or less per acre. There's no federal cleanup requirement.

House critics call the law a relic and want legislation to impose an 8% gross royalty on hard-rock minerals taken from public lands.

The law also would end the cheap $2.50- to $5-an-acre sales of public land, and demand tougher reclamation once mining ends.

And it would earmark certain fees toward a fund to help defray the growing costs — up to $72 billion — of cleaning up abandoned mines.

More than 3 million acres of public land have been sold and are now the source for 85% of U.S. gold, silver and other metals. The other 15% — about $2 billion worth — is still mined from federal lands.

Senators in May passed an industry-backed plan that would levy a 2% royalty on net mineral values, after mining expenses. It leaves reclamation mandates up to states.

Industry says an 8% royalty would

## Royalties would pay for cleanup

A plan under consideration to reform the Mining Act of 1872 would charge mining companies royalties for minerals extracted from public lands. A portion of the royalties would be returned to states for land reclamation and cleanup. Estimated amount each state would get a year:

| State | Amount (in millions) |
|---|---|
| Nevada | $52.2 |
| Arizona | $42.8 |
| Colorado | $15.8 |
| Utah | $12.4 |
| Idaho | $11.3 |
| Montana | $10.6 |
| California | $9.7 |
| New Mexico | $8.5 |
| Washington | $3.9 |
| Wyoming | $3.0 |
| Oregon | $0.4 |

Source: Mineral Policy Center

make it tough for many to stay in business here. "We won't be competitive," says Michael Brown of The Gold Institute, a trade group.

This war of words has turned to economic volleys:

▶ Two University of Nevada-Reno economists estimate the House bill will cost Nevada nearly 1,040 jobs and $61 million in state revenues. Nevada's 13,000 mine workers earn an average $38,751 yearly.

▶ A University of Montana economist study says the House bill will mean 1,200 new jobs in the West — many of them in reclaiming abandoned mine sites. It says only three of every 10,000 Western jobs are mining on federal lands.

Philip Hocker of environmental group Mineral Policy Center says reform is long overdue.

"America needs (reform) to force mining companies to make fair payment, to run a clean mine and to clean up the mess they've been leaving behind for more than a century," he says.

USA TODAY, NOVEMBER 16, 1993

# Diamonds, Rubies, and Emeralds

## Purpose

To grow crystals under different conditions and to identify their characteristics.

## Background

Ancient societies valued gemstones for their long-lasting beauty. For centuries, gems have been used as money, in worship, and as symbols of wealth and power.

Mining these gems required moving tremendous amounts of soil and rock. The amount of earth that has to be moved has changed little over the centuries, but the equipment used to mine gems has greatly improved. Modern machinery and explosives make it possible to move more rock with fewer people and in much less time.

Today, gems for industrial and personal use are not only mined from the ground, they are also made synthetically—manufactured from raw materials. Synthetic gems were first manufactured in the late 1800s, and they became very popular. Today, even professional gemologists have difficulty telling high-quality synthetic gems from their natural twins.

In the 1930s, the demand for synthetic gems grew so great that it sometimes became unprofitable to mine natural gems. Gem mining in the United States slowed, and many mines closed. As the demand for real gems has again increased, however, some of these closed mines have been reopened.

You are a chemist for a company that develops useful industrial products from natural and human-made gems and crystals. This morning you were asked to evaluate the crystallization characteristics of some solutions. It is hoped that the information you gather can be applied to the development of a new synthetic crystal to be used in medical lasers.

## Materials

**For each student (Part 1):**
- Crystal-model cutouts (from the teacher)
- Crystal Identification Key (from the teacher)
- Colored pencils or markers
- Scissors
- Tape or glue

**For each pair (Part 2):**
- 2 pair of goggles
- Petri dishes
- Room-temperature solutions (from the teacher)
- 1 warmed solution (from the teacher)
- Eyedropper
- Stereoscope or microscope
- Labels and marker
- 100-ml beaker
- Room temperature or cold microscope slides
- Warmed microscope slides
- Fax cover sheet (from the teacher)

## Procedure

### Part 1

1. Color the crystal models as indicated.
2. Cut out the colored models and label each model with its shape name.
3. Glue or tape each shape together so the tabs are on the inside of the completed structures.
4. Use the Crystal Identification Key to label each crystal model with its chemical name.

### Part 2

1. Be sure to wear goggles at all times!
2. With a partner, select a bottle of crystal-growing solution from your teacher.
3. Use a marker to label a petri dish with the code number of the solution you select. Pour 20 milliliters of the solution into the labeled petri dish.
4. Allow the liquid to evaporate and crystals to form.
5. (Optional) Your teacher may allow you to grow more than one kind of crystal. If so, repeat steps 2 through 4 with each solution.
6. Design a chart in which you can record color, shape, size, luster, and any other observations or comments about the crystals. Record this information for all of the different crystals grown.
7. Observe the crystals under a stereoscope or microscope.

## Part 3

1. Obtain an unknown saturated solution from your teacher. Use an eyedropper to place one drop on a cool or cold microscope slide. Use the stereoscope or microscope to observe the crystals as they grow. Record your observations.

2. Repeat procedure 1, using the corresponding heated unknown on a warmed slide.

3. With the help of the Crystal Identification Key and your observations, try to identify the unknown substance.

## Part 4

Your boss is in a hurry to see the data and a summary of your findings. Prepare a one-page facsimile (fax) to send to your home office in New York. In your fax, identify the unknown substance and state reasons supporting your identification. Also compare and contrast the results of the slowly grown crystals (in the petri dishes and on the cooled slide) with the rapidly grown crystals (on the heated slide). Does the speed of crystallization change the crystals in any way? If the crystals have identifiable shapes, be sure to name them.

# Gemstones

## Natural Gemstones

A natural gemstone is mineral, stone, or organic matter. After it has been cut and polished or otherwise treated, it becomes a gem. Gems are used in jewelry, in ornaments, and sometimes in industry.

A precious gemstone has beauty, durability, and rarity. A semiprecious gemstone has only one or two of these qualities. Generally classified as precious stones are diamond, corundum (ruby and sapphire), beryl (emerald and aquamarine), topaz, and opal. All other gemstones are usually classified as semiprecious.

Gemstones do not form ore deposits in the normal sense. Gems, when present at all, tend to be scattered sparsely throughout a large body of rock. They may crystallize as small aggregates or fill veins and small cavities.

Even stream-gravel concentrations tend to be small—a few stones in each of several bedrock cracks or potholes or gravel deposits in a stream bed.

Most gemstones are found in igneous rocks and alluvial gravels, but sedimentary and metamorphic rocks may also contain gem materials.

## Organic Gemstones

In addition to mineral gemstones, there are four organic gemstone groups: amber, coral, jet, and pearl. Organic gemstones are highly valued for their beauty and rarity. They are more easily scratched or broken than gemstones from minerals.

Amber is the hard fossilized resin or sap of ancient trees. It does not have a crystalline structure. Sometimes it contains the remains of ancient insects that were trapped in the sap before it hardened. Amber played a major role in *Jurassic Park*. It can be mined and is sometimes even gathered on seashores.

Coral is the remains of the skeletons of billions of tiny marine animals that live together in colonies. Coral reefs, barrier reefs, and atolls are created by these coral-producing animals. Coral is formed mainly from calcite (calcium carbonate) or conchiolin, a branching organic substance.

Jet is made up of carbon and various hydrocarbon compounds. It is a compact, velvet-black coal that can be polished.

A pearl can form within a mollusk, such as an oyster, or in various clams and mussels. The mollusk deposits a substance called *nacre* around an irritant, such as a grain of sand, that has entered the organism. This coated irritant becomes a pearl. Pearl-bearing mollusks are found in both salt water and freshwater.

# Mining Engineer

**RICHARD LOCK
CHIEF MINING ENGINEER,
DIAMONDS
KENNECOTT MINING
COMPANY OF CANADA
YELLOWKNIFE, NORTHWEST
TERRITORIES, CANADA**

A security guard X-rays us every time we leave the diamond mine. Diamonds are precious and expensive, so diamond-mining companies must protect themselves against possible theft by their own workers.

Sometimes workers will try to steal diamonds by swallowing them. The diamonds show up on the X-ray even inside the body.

I am the chief mining engineer for Kennecott Mining Company of Canada. I am currently involved in a mining exploration more than 300 kilometers (185 miles) north of the town of Yellowknife in Canada's Northwest Territory. I have also worked as a mining engineer in a diamond mine in South Africa.

In high school, I was good in math and science. I was also interested in geology. I now wish I had devoted more time to writing. An engineer writes many reports. Good writing skills are important.

After earning my mining degree, I was eager to work as an engineer. But my first few years at the mine were frustrating. I had to do the hard physical work of a miner: drilling, blasting, and unloading rock.

I finally worked my way up to engineering. I learned that the hard, manual work was essential to understanding my job as an engineer. It was important to learn the basics in a real mine after studying about it in school.

My typical day is spent in the office rather than in the mine. I start work about 6:30 A.M. and finish around 5:00 P.M. When I arrive, I review what has happened since I was there the day before. The mine operates 24 hours a day. I then discuss the plans for the day with my coworkers. We decide what needs to be done where and who should do the work.

I use a computer every day. The mining data we collect are placed in databases that we use to analyze the progress of our work. For example, we have a database with information about production. We study how many tons of rock have been removed from the mine. We record where in the mine the rocks were collected. The computer calculates the ratio of diamonds to rock. We use this information in deciding which sections to mine for the most diamonds.

I go into the mine two or three days a week for about three hours each time. When I return to my office, I write my report and complete my analysis for the day on my computer.

Most diamond mines are not very deep. Our mine in South Africa was about 760 meters (2,500 feet) deep. The temperature at that depth is about 21°C (70°F). It's very comfortable. However, the deeper you go toward the center of the earth, the hotter it becomes. At around 3,650 meters (12,000 feet), the temperature can reach as high as 50°C (120°F).

When we enter a mine, we wear coveralls, steel-toed boots, a hard hat, gloves, and eye protection. Mufflers protect our ears from the noise of the machines. A cap lamp helps us see where we are going.

We also carry rescue packs. They provide air in case of fire or poisonous gas such as carbon monoxide in the mine. I take a two-liter bottle of frozen water with me. As it melts during the day, I have fresh, cold water to drink. I also take my lunch. There are places to brew coffee underground. It is actually quite civilized down there.

Diamond mines are generally located on old volcanoes. Diamonds are found in *kimberlite*. Kimberlite is magma that cooled inside the tube-like part of the volcano. Diamonds can be removed easily from the kimberlite by soaking the rock in a dense liquid. Kimberlite floats to the top, and diamonds sink to the bottom.

The concentration of diamonds in mines is incredibly low. Diamonds do not run in veins as do gold and silver. They are scattered throughout the kimberlite. Some areas of the kimberlite have more diamonds, but other areas have less.

We mine about 10,900 metric tons (12,000 short tons) of kimberlite per day. Yet, in all that tonnage, we may find only enough diamonds to fill your cupped hands. Most of the diamonds are small. We usually find five diamonds per day that are larger than 10 karats. A 10-karat diamond is about the size of the fingernail on your little finger.

There are many questions to answer when deciding whether or not to open an abandoned diamond mine. First, how much is the rock worth? How many diamonds might the mine produce? What grade of diamonds did the

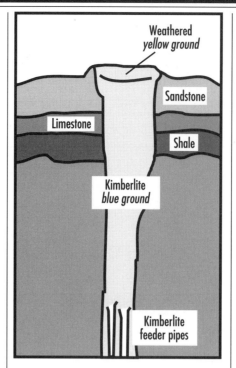

*This is a cross section of a kimberlite pipe where diamonds are often found.*

mine produce before it closed? Is the mine flooded? Rainwater and underground streams seep into most mines. Unless you keep pumping water out, they become flooded. I have seen it take two years to pump out the water.

Toxic chemicals are not used in processing kimberlite for diamonds, so regulatory problems are usually few. However, a supply of water is necessary for running the mine and for drinking. Most mines are remote—some are in desert areas—so you have to have a water source.

Next, realize that opening an abandoned mine can be like opening a new mine. You will want to replace any old, rusty equipment left in the mine with new, high-tech equipment. That can be expensive, but safety and efficiency are important. You will need an elevator shaft, rock-crushing equipment, and conveyor belts to move the rock.

Pumps are needed to remove water. They are also needed to pump water for air-conditioning systems, life support, and other uses.

Finally, you need workers and housing and supplies for them. You may have to fly the workers into the mining area. They usually work the mines for periods of six weeks at a time and then take short vacations.

Our diamond mine in South Africa had about 2,000 employees. About half worked in mining offices on the surface. The other half worked underground. Much of the work is mechanized. Most workers nowadays are highly trained.

The types of jobs vary. For example, besides miners, engineers, and geologists, there are mechanics who maintain and repair the underground diesel-powered vehicles and other equipment. People are needed to run the elevators in the mine shafts. Other workers recover the diamonds. Then there are sorters who separate diamonds into different grades and sizes. And, of course, there are security people to prevent stealing.

Working in a mine is not an easy life. Most mines are in remote areas. There is not much to do except work. Those who work underground do not see sunlight for eight or more hours a day. It is not easy work, but it's quite rewarding.

# Gold, Silver, and Copper: What Are They Worth Today?

Where do you find the current prices of gold, silver, and copper? Check the business section of your daily newspaper. Look near the New York Stock Exchange (NYSE) and NASDAQ listings.

You will usually find the going rates for gold, silver, and perhaps copper near the foreign-exchange listings. In some newspapers, these are listed as metals under commodity prices.

In the *New York Times*, metals are listed under Cash Prices. Metals also have listings under World Gold and London Metals. In *USA Today*, gold and silver are listed under Key Indicators and then under Commodities. In early 1995, gold was selling for about $375 per troy ounce, and silver was going for about $4.75 per troy ounce. How does that compare to the prices today?

| Average Mineral Prices 1975–1992 | | | | |
|---|---|---|---|---|
| Year | Gold (dollar/oz) | Silver (dollar/oz) | Copper (cents/lb) | Zinc (cents/lb) |
| 1975 | 161 | 4.42 | 64 | 39.0 |
| 1976 | 125 | 4.35 | 70 | 37.0 |
| 1977 | 148 | 4.62 | 67 | 34.4 |
| 1978 | 194 | 5.40 | 66 | 31.0 |
| 1979 | 308 | 11.09 | 92 | 37.3 |
| 1980 | 613 | 20.63 | 101 | 37.4 |
| 1981 | 460 | 10.52 | 84 | 44.6 |
| 1982 | 376 | 7.95 | 73 | 38.5 |
| 1983 | 424 | 11.44 | 77 | 41.4 |
| 1984 | 361 | 8.14 | 67 | 48.6 |
| 1985 | 318 | 6.14 | 67 | 40.4 |
| 1986 | 368 | 5.47 | 66 | 38.0 |
| 1987 | 448 | 7.01 | 83 | 41.9 |
| 1988 | 438 | 6.54 | 120 | 60.2 |
| 1989 | 383 | 5.50 | 131 | 82.0 |
| 1990 | 385 | 4.82 | 123 | 74.6 |
| 1991 | 363 | 4.04 | 109 | 52.8 |
| 1992 | 350 | 4.00 | 107 | 59.0 |

# The Future of the Copper Market

How does the future look for the price of copper? Mining has been profitable in the United States in part because the Mining Law of 1872 allows mining companies to buy public land for as little as $2.50 an acre. But that may change soon.

Members of Congress may change the law. They may demand payment from mining companies for the metals and minerals removed from government land, which would add to the cost of mining. Congress may also decide not to give mining companies land patents. This could make banks reluctant to loan money to mining companies.

Because of uncertainty about what will happen, many U.S. mining companies have begun prospecting in South America. For now, the climate for prospecting is better in South America than here.

There are several other important things to consider when thinking about future copper prices. Fiber optics, such as those used in new telephone cables, are new competition for the copper industry. The competition can influence the demand for copper. Copper might be discovered in Brazil or another South American country. Foreign copper may flood the U.S. copper market. Could any of these factors bring the price of copper down?

There is another factor that may influence copper prices. Developing countries are beginning to provide electricity and telephone services to more and more of their citizens. What do you predict will happen to the price of copper if the demand for it increases?

## KEY INDICATORS WEDNESDAY

| Indicator | WED. | Change from Tues. | 6 mos. |
|---|---|---|---|
| **STOCKS** | | | |
| S&P 500 | 605.94 | -1.0% | 11.4% |
| S&P Midcap | 212.45 | 0.3% | 7.3% |
| Dow industrials | 5059.32 | -1.0% | 11.3% |
| Dow transports | 2008.38 | 0.6% | 16.0% |
| Dow utilities | 221.77 | -.07% | 11.0% |
| NYSE composite | 323.61 | -0.6% | 11.0% |
| Amex mkt. value | 534.50 | 0.5% | 8.2% |
| Nasdaq comp. | 1025.27 | -0.1% | 10.3% |
| H&Q growth(tech) | 2056.77 | 0.8% | 22.9% |
| Russel 2000 | 308.83 | 0.9% | 9.2% |
| Wilshire 5000 | 5943.05 | -.05% | 11.3% |
| **BONDS** | | | |
| Long T-bonds[1] | 6561.96 | -0.2% | 7.8% |
| Inter. T-bonds[1] | 4583.13 | -0.1% | 4.0% |
| Muni., 2-yr. yld.[2] | 4.05% | -0.7% | -6.7% |
| Muni., 10-yr. yld.[2] | 4.95% | -0.6% | 18.1% |

1- Lehman Bros. total return indexes

| Indicator | WED. | Change from Tues. | 6 mos. |
|---|---|---|---|
| **MUTUAL FUNDS** | | | |
| Lipper growth index | 4045.86 | -0.2% | 8.4% |
| Lipper small co. index | 465.13 | 0.6% | 10.7% |
| Lipper international | 481.03 | 1.0% | 3.9% |
| Lipper grth. & income | 3840.61 | -0.3% | 9.8% |
| **COMMODITIES** | | | |
| Lt. sweet crude oil | 18.97 | -0.1% | 8.4% |
| Platinum | 407.60 | unch. | -7.9% |
| Gold | 388.80 | 0.4% | -0.4% |
| Silver | 5.125 | 0.5% | -5.6% |
| CRB | 245.43 | unch. | 3.3% |
| Wheat | 5.015 bu. | -1.8% | 26.1% |
| Corn | 3.545 bu. | 3.3% | 25.7% |
| Soybeans | 7.323 bu. | -1.1% | 20.9% |
| Cattle | 67.07 | -0.3% | 6.0% |
| Hogs | 47.55 | -1.1% | -4.9% |

2 - PSA/Bloomberg Municipal Bond Indexes

USA TODAY, DECEMBER 21, 1995

# Mineral Policy Center

**JIM LYON, VICE PRESIDENT FOR POLICY
MINERAL POLICY CENTER
WASHINGTON, D.C.**

The Mineral Policy Center is a national environmental organization dedicated to mineral policy and research. We put out a lot of information on the environmental and physical impact of mining policy. We are an advocacy group that pushes for social change.

The Mineral Policy Center is not an anti-mining organization, but we do feel that the mining policies in this country, and mining industry practices have a very long way to go to be consistently responsible. We also believe that the regulation of the mining industry is far behind the technological practices of the industry and the environmental and community impacts that it creates.

As Vice President for Policy, I supervise program and policy work here at the center. My job is a combination of several different tasks. I oversee the publication of the various fact sheets and reports we generate throughout the year. I handle press questions and actually call reporters to get them interested in covering the mining story. Also I am the Center's chief lobbyist. I spend a lot of time on Capitol Hill working on mining legislation. I also work with organizations in communities across the country that are impacted by mining. Together we develop

***Copper Mining in Arizona*** PHILIP M. HOCKER/MINERAL POLICY CENTER

common strategies for pushing reform.

There is no typical day for me. A lot of what I do is juggling my various efforts. At any given time, we are working on several projects. Right now we're writing a book on mining's impact on water quality. It should be released in the next couple of months. Now there are all sorts of details to check on. . ... How are the writers doing? Is the editing process set up? Are the photographs in? These are the nuts and bolts of my job. On any given day, I can get as many as a dozen telephone calls from the press. Reporters often call with questions related to a mining story they're writing.

If Congress is in session, and things are happening on the Hill, my whole day may be spent making calls and visiting Congress; or I could be writing factsheets about a piece of legis-

lation that is moving through Congress. I also attend meetings with other strategists and regulatory officials. My days vary. They are interesting, but they can drive me a little crazy at times.

I've always been interested in social change issues. Soon after I got out of college, I worked in a small business. I wasn't finding the commercial world very fulfilling, when I was handed an opportunity to work on a coal mining issue. My first visit to Central Appalachia was a life-defining trip for me. It was a region I had never seen before. It was quite chilling to see the impact of coal mining on the people down there. I didn't expect it, but that experience has kept me in this business for sixteen or seventeen years. I've always been concerned about environmental issues, but those that involve human struggles are especially interesting and fulfilling.

➤ continued on page 44

➤ continued from page 43

I have a political science background. I don't have a science major, but the geometry and chemistry classes that I took help me in my work. I wish I had more. If you want to get into the environmental field, a science background is an excellent tool. If you are interested in public policy work, I recommend that you specialize in something. If you are interested in mining or any other environmental topic, get the educational background you need to really know the subject. Then, get involved. It's tough to get a job without experience. Try volunteering or interning at an organization, or join a local environmental group. We always need volunteers. Some of the best advocates I work with are volunteers. They are often as good as people who get paid fulltime.

We focus a lot on the issue of abandoned mines. In fact we wrote a report on the problem of abandoned mines about two

or three years ago. As you think about reopening an abandoned mine, keep in mind the environmental and public impacts of the existing mine. A lot of good can be done when a mine is reopened. Many abandoned mines are just sitting out there without much hope of ever being cleaned up. These abandoned mines are often threats to public health and safety.

Old underground mines that still have an opening, are especially dangerous. People get killed at these sites every year. Reopening one of these mines can be a desirable thing to do.

Other problems, from scars on the landscape to severe water quality problems, can sometimes be cleaned up when a mine is reopened. However, there are many examples of companies carelessly moving into an area with big mining equipment, and making a bad situation horrendous.

A lot of mining today is chemical mining. Ores that con-

**PHILIP M. HOCKER/MINERAL POLICY CENTER** *This copper mine, like many others, is using dump leaching for an increasing amount of its production. This practice, while economical and energy efficient, poses serious risks to groundwater from leakage of acid and heavy metal contaminated solutions into underlying aquifers.*

tain valuable minerals are first ground up and put in piles. Then piles are sprayed with a solution such as cyanide. The cyanide percolates through the piles and dissolves the gold or other minerals. This can be done safely, but when you're talking about mining on a very large scale, or when a company cuts corners or makes mistakes, this technique can create a new problem that was not there before. Cyanide can leak through a liner and enter the groundwater; or it can overflow and kill nearby streams. Unfortunately we have examples of both of these things happening every year. I don't criticize the entire mining industry. In many cases, remining an area is a good way to clean things up. It has to be done carefully and it should not be done everywhere.

**Gold Mining in Montana.**
*A request to double the size of this gold mining operation is being opposed by environmental groups because there is no adequate reclamation plan and the mine's impact on water resources has not been considered. Groundwater is less than 30 meters (100 feet) below surface.*

**MINERAL POLICY CENTER**

# Remains of a Gold Rush

For those who did not arrive early in 1849, the pickings were slim. Most of the available surface gold deposits had already been claimed. This loose and easily mined gold was in a form called *placer deposits*. Placer deposits are concentrations of gold caused by the erosion, disintegration, or decomposition of rock originally surrounding the gold. In the gold-bearing California countryside, prospectors looked for placer gold where coarse sands and gravel had accumulated.

Prospectors built various contraptions to remove gold that had been overlooked by earlier miners. Devices such as the cradle, the long tom, and the sluice box provided methods to process greater volumes of water, dirt, and gravel in less time. They allowed miners to remove even the smallest specks of gold.

The earliest placer miners found deposits of placer gold in dust, flake, and nugget form. But the supply of placer gold was soon depleted and hard-rock digging began. In time, large-scale mining tore up enormous slices of California landscape. Valleys were ravaged as mining machines ripped into the countryside.

In 1851, the entire 30-mile length of the American River was temporarily shifted from its original channel. The river's diversion permitted miners to scour stream beds for gold.

One of the more earth-wrenching methods of mining was using streams of water. This hydraulic mining technique sprayed pressurized water. It could dislodge nearly 50,000 tons of gravel in a day, leaving behind deep holes and piles of rubble. To get at gold-bearing quartz veins buried deep in the ground, miners sunk shafts and brought rock up through them. They could then crush and treat the rock to remove the gold.

In 1852 alone, miners extracted about $81 million worth of gold. They mined more than $220 million in gold over the five years following the discovery at Sutter's mill. But by the end of 1852, most of the easily found gold had already been mined. That year is considered the end of the great California Gold Rush.

The gold that made its way downstream to Sutter's mill had originated in the Sierra Nevada. Quartz veins were identified as the source.

Some who had profited from the rush of 1849 continued their quest for gold. Others, less fortunate or bankrupt, tried to put their lives back together.

Ghost towns now sit as spooky reminders of the California Gold Rush—the greatest gold rush in the history of the United States. And it all began with James Marshall, a carpenter, stooping over and picking up a small piece of gold worth no more than 50 cents.

*Miners used jets of water to dislodge gravel that might hide gold.* PHOTO FROM THE CALIFORNIA DEPARTMENT OF PARKS AND RECREATION.

# Fax It ASAP

## Purpose

To classify and identify igneous rocks.

## Background

You have just received a phone call from your company's operations manager. She needs your help. Two investors, Sid A. Mentry and Matt O. Morphic, visited the mine site and picked up an unknown rock. They want the rock identified immediately. This is a job for a geologist, but the company geologist is on assignment in Africa.

Your state geologist knows the area and is sending by overnight mail a set of igneous rocks to help you. Along with the labeled samples, the geologist is sending an identification key.

When the envelope arrives, the operations manager hands it to you and tells you to get to work. When you open the envelope, you notice the sample rocks are not labeled. At first, you think this will not be a problem. You will just use the key to identify the rocks. But you don't find anything else when you dig through the package. The key and the rock labels have been lost or forgotten.

Now what? "Do the best you can," the operations manager says. "I'll call the state geologist and have the key faxed to you. Good Luck!"

## Materials

**Per pair:**
- Unknown rock
- Rock samples in envelope
- Hand lens
- Masking tape
- Marker
- Stereo microscope (optional)
- File folder

## Procedure

You are running out of time, so you have decided to develop some kind of classification system to help you make sense out of the rocks you received.

1. Study the rocks and list some criteria you can use to sort them into logical groups.
2. Draw a table that shows your criteria; then use the table to classify the rock samples.
3. Use masking tape and the marker to number labels for the samples. Numbers will help you keep track of them. You can also use the numbers on the table you develop.
4. When you finish, your table will be a permanent record of the rocks that belong in each group and the criteria you used to separate the groups. Use your table to identify the unknown rock from the mine site.
5. Now ask the operations manager (your teacher) whether the fax has arrived. If it has, use this information to make a new table and try again to identify the mine sample. Do not throw away the old table.
6. If a second fax arrives, you may use it to make one last table and change your rock identification if necessary.

## Conclusion

Collect the tables that demonstrate your attempts at classifying the rocks. In a folder, place your best classification table on top and earlier attempts underneath it.

Also enclose a letter to the two investors thanking them for their interest in your company. Be sure to include your identification of the rock they sent.

# California to Australia and Beyond

As the chance of striking it rich in California declined, a new gold rush was about to begin. A miner from Australia was having little luck finding gold in California. He realized that the gold-bearing rocks of California were similar to rocks he knew well in Australia.

He headed home to seek his fortune. In 1851, he found gold in New South Wales in the southeast corner of Australia. Gold diggers flocked in from California, Britain, China, and other corners of the world.

The first prospectors found nuggets in streams. Sometimes they found nuggets just lying on the ground. What is said to be one of the largest chunks of gold ever found was discovered there. It weighed 2,285 ounces.

Again, it was not long before the more easily found gold was gone. Then prospectors had to dig as deep as 200 feet to find more. It was hard work digging through both soil and rock.

Most prospectors were young, single men. But sometimes whole families worked together. School was not mandatory in those days. Even six- and ten-year-old children worked beside their parents. They worked in streams and down in mine shafts.

Before long, prospectors were off and running again. Other gold rushes drew gold seekers to New Zealand, Alaska, British Columbia, Nevada, Colorado, and South Africa.

Gold fever is not a disease of the distant past. As recently as the early 1980s, all the evils of earlier gold rushes descended upon South America. As in the past, it was a nightmare for natives of the area.

The worst is still taking place in Peru today. In villages in the Andes, children are recruited by mining companies. Children as young as 12 years old leave home hoping to strike it rich by panning for gold in the Amazon region. Companies there are exploiting at least several thousand children. For only $2.60 a day, they are working 10 to 12 hours a day. Working conditions are terrible, and the children are fed only rice, potatoes, yucca root, and water. They are overworked and undernourished. They sleep outside at night. Many children die from tuberculosis, malaria, and parasites—the results of unsanitary conditions and lack of health care. Using children for heavy labor is against Peruvian law, but the laws are not being enforced.

When you and your team set up your mining company, understand the local laws. Also think about the impact your operations will have on the environment and the people in the community.

## FROM CALIFORNIA.

### ARRIVAL OF THE STAR OF THE WEST.

### $920,000 IN GOLD.

#### Interesting News from the Pacific

The United States mail steamer *Star of the West*, Capt. Gray, arrived at this port last evening, from Aspinwall March 5, bringing the California mails and gold of Feb. 19. The amount of gold by this arrival is small, being but $924,000. The news has been in part anticipated, as usual, by the Overland Mail and the Tehuantepec arrival.

The *Star of the West* connected with the *Golden Age*, which vessel was boarded off Manzanilla by a boat from the United States sloop-of-war *Vandalia*. The officers and crew of the *Vandalia* were all well.

The United States frigate *Roanoke* was at Aspinwall. All well on board.

On the 9th inst., latitude 24° 10', longitude 81° 58', the *Star of the West*, passed ship *J. Morton*. On the 10th inst., latitude 27° 30', longitude 79° 50', passed schooner *J. H. Houston*. On the 12th, at 3 1/2 P.M., passed bark *Orlando*, of Boston, steering north.

We are indebted to Purser Patterson, of the *Star of the West*, and to Wells, Fargo & Co.'s Express, and Furrman & Co., for favors.

The following is the gold list of the *Star of the West:*

| | | | |
|---|---|---|---|
| Wells, Fargo & Co | $197,500 | J. B. Newton & Co | $12,329 |
| Am. Ex. Bank | 104,000 | Crocker & Warren | 12,171 |
| W. Hetler & Co. | 91,459 | T. B. Wales & Co. | 12,000 |
| E. Kelly & Co. | 50,000 | Janson, Bond & Co. | 11,000 |
| W. Hoge, & Co. | 46,000 | A. Hardy & Co. | 10,000 |
| W. T. Coleman & Co. | 45,750 | Jennings & Brewster | 10,000 |
| James Patrick | 40,000 | P. Naylor | 10,000 |
| Freeman & Co. | 39,900 | R. L. Maitland & Co. | 8,000 |
| Howes & Crowell | 33,000 | Butcher & Brother | 7,200 |
| Taffee, McCahill & Co. | 28,000 | Bates & Co. | 6,846 |
| Order | 22,000 | J. G. Parker & Son | 6,000 |
| Wm. Sellgman & Co. | 20,000 | C. W. Crosby | 5,000 |
| J. B. Wier | 15,193 | H. L. Ritch & Co. | 4,000 |
| R. Meader & O. Adams | 15,000 | Turner Bros. | 4,000 |
| Clark & Wilbur | 15,000 | C. H. Cummings | 3,000 |
| J. H. Coghill | 17,284 | T. J. Hand & Co. | 3,000 |
| Howland & Aspinwall | 12,845 | S. G. Reed & Co. | 2,700 |
| | | Total | $920,177 |

FROM ASPINWALL.

| | | | |
|---|---|---|---|
| Panama R. R. Co. | $8,000 | S. Lansburg & Bro. | 1,573 |
| Provor & Colgate | 3,380 | Total | $12,953 |

The New York Times, March 14, 1859

# Prospecting from Space

Looking for gold can be a sky-high enterprise! Geologists are using satellites circling the earth to spot locations where gold might be found.

Geologists now use satellite imagery routinely. Pictures taken by satellites are useful for many different purposes. One use is locating the earth's resources, such as oil, gas, and minerals. As satellites sweep over tracts of land, they take pictures. They scan earth's surface, sensing visible light and other parts of the electromagnetic spectrum. Energy from different parts of the electromagnetic spectrum carries with it different kinds of information.

Satellites save time and money. It is very expensive to send a team of people to survey large areas of ground in the hope of finding valuable minerals. One satellite image can be used to examine hundreds of square kilometers at a time.

*Satellite image of Malpais, New Mexico.*
COURTESY OF EOSAT.

These images help geologists identify surface features that indicate where a valuable mineral such as gold may be found.

Several years ago, Japanese geologists used satellite images to explore New Guinea. They saw what looked like geological structures associated with gold. When geologists went to the site, they discovered they were right.

The Japanese team saved millions of dollars and many years of time, thanks to the satellite images.

Searching for valuable minerals is very competitive. Sending a lot of people to scour the landscape can tip off other interested people. Satellite images let you study a site without anyone else knowing!

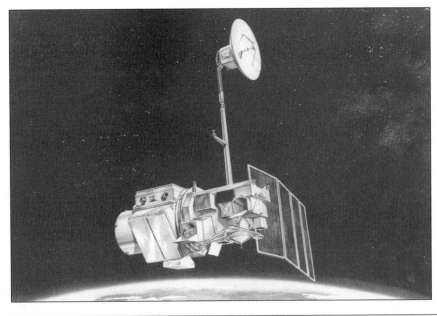

*Artist's rendition of Landsat Satellite orbiting the earth at 640 kilometers.*
NASA

# Mining Asteroids: A Chip off the Old Rock

There are thousands of giant boulders flying through space. These heavenly hunks of rock are called *asteroids*. An average asteroid is about 10 kilometers (6 miles) in diameter and is loaded with minerals. Some believe asteroids are a virtual gold mine in space.

Most of these tiny bodies are in a zone called the *asteroid belt*. The belt is a circle of asteroids orbiting the Sun between the orbits of Mars and Jupiter. Nobody is quite sure why these rocks are there. Are they leftover from a broken-up planet? Or could they be material that did not clump together to form a larger body?

There are also about 5,000 asteroids whose orbits bring them closer to the inner planets. These bodies are called *near-earth asteroids*.

Scientists believe the rocky bodies carry material that has changed little since their formation. Learning more about asteroids allows us to peer back billions of years—to the earliest days of the solar system's formation.

Asteroids are a motherlode of minerals. It is already known that some carry alloys of iron, nickel, and cobalt. Asteroids also carry titanium, magnesium, manganese, carbon, sulfur, and various other metals and nonmetals. Some asteroids may hold small percentages of water—a valuable resource in space.

You could say the first prospector to survey asteroids

This is an artist's conception of what it might be like to mine an asteroid. **COURTESY OF PAMELA LEE**

has already been sent. The *Galileo* spacecraft, en route to Jupiter, flew by two asteroids: Gaspra in 1991 and Ida in 1993.

In 1996, the *Near Earth Asteroid Rendezvous* (NEAR) spacecraft is slated for launch. This craft will reach the asteroid Eros in late 1998. The NEAR spacecraft will orbit the asteroid for nearly a year. Instruments on the probe will scan the asteroid in detail.

Eventually, astronauts might visit asteroids. They could collect samples for return to Earth. After the first surveys of asteroids are complete, could these space rocks be mined?

In the future, mining camps might be set up on asteroids to extract their minerals and metals. If so, these resources could be processed to build habitats and other structures in space. Asteroid-mining camps could also supply other resources to support the mining operations.

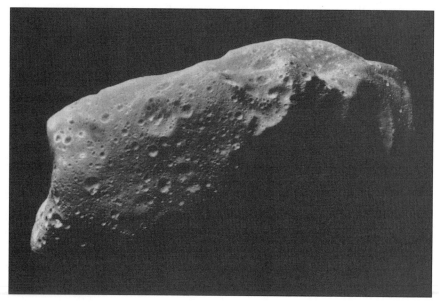

Asteroid 243 Ida is a mosaic of five image frames taken by the Galileo spacecraft from a distance of approximately 3500 kilometers. **NASA**

# Mining the Moon and Mars

"There's gold in them thar hills!" is an old saying. But for future space travelers, it could mean hitting celestial paydirt on the moon and Mars.

The first human prospectors of another world were the *Apollo* astronauts. Teams of *Apollo* explorers landed on the moon between 1969 and 1972. They took hammers, collecting bags, and even drills to sample the lunar surface. Six different sites were sampled.

Although they did not find gold, they found other riches. More than 40 percent of the materials scooped up contained oxygen joined with other elements to form compounds called *oxides*. The moon samples typically contained silicon (20 percent), aluminum (14 percent), and iron (4 percent). Titanium, manganese, magnesium, and chromium were also detected in smaller amounts.

Future bases on the moon may be able to use these materials to make buildings, rocket fuel, and air to breathe! What might future prospecting on the moon uncover? Some scientists believe water may be discovered on the airless moon in craters that are never exposed to sunlight. If water is found, it would be priceless to people working on the moon—just as valuable as gold on Earth!

Although human prospectors have not yet gone to Mars, robots landed there in 1976. Using special equipment, two *Viking* robots analyzed Martian

*Mining the moon for oxygen, aluminum, iron, and titanium could be profitable in the future.* LOCKHEED MISSILES AND SPACE CO.

soil. Each robot lander used a mechanical arm to dig into the surface of Mars. Many of the same minerals found on Earth were found on Mars.

The reddish-colored soil of Mars is caused by iron-bearing rocks that have reacted with oxygen to become rust. Wind erosion has cut into surface rocks, distributing particles of rock over the planet. Astronomers can see sand dunes in some areas of Mars. Feldspars, clays, iron oxides, sulfates, and other minerals were studied at the *Viking* landing spots. The deserts of Mars appear to be similar to the deserts of Earth.

Could there be valuable mineral deposits on Mars? It is too early to tell. However, Mars does have volcanoes. It has also been struck by meteorites. It appears that considerable amounts of water have swept across the Martian surface in the past.

Those same conditions have helped form valuable mineral deposits on Earth.

*This view of Mars was taken by the Viking Orbiter from 2,500 kilometers away.* NASA

# Technology Education: Servo or Not Servo

## Purpose

To design and construct a robotics device that will assist in the mining of minerals.

## Background

Space exploration has increased our knowledge of the "what," the "what if," and the "how to." Robots have helped with that exploration. Robots have also helped in other areas of engineering and manufacturing.

When we think of robots, we often think of R2D2 or C3PO from *Star Wars*. But not all robotics devices are humanoids. Since the 1960s and 70s, manufacturers have been faced with high energy costs, foreign competition, and increased worker reluctance to perform repetitive and hazardous jobs. Robots have played an important role in turning around failing industries. Robotic devices perform assembly tasks, handle materials, weld, perform machine operations, and so on.

Scientists are using walking robots to study remote and dangerous sites. "Dante II," one of these robots, has been used to study Mount Spurr in Alaska. Dante II has taken pictures and measured the gases, temperatures, and other properties within the crater of this active volcano.

Your task as the Research and Development Department of the Dig 'Em Deep Mining Company is to construct a robotics device that will help mine valuable minerals from beneath the earth's surface.

## Materials

**Per group:**

- Construction materials (approved by the instructor)
- 6 to 8 syringes (6–20 cc)
- 1/8-inch-diameter clear plastic tubing
- Adhesive
- Springs (optional)
- Eye screws (optional)
- Gears (optional)
- Wooden dowels (optional)
- Fasteners
- Rubber bands (optional)
- Graph paper
- Scissors and/or mat knife
- bearing from Lazy Susan (optional)

## Procedures

1. Investigate robotics.
2. Design and construct a robotics device that will perform one of the tasks in mining (for example, drilling, scraping, digging, picking, or moving)
3. Make appropriate sketches needed to build the device.
4. Using graph paper, draw any patterns needed.
5. Gather all appropriate materials.
6. Safely use any tools and/or machines approved by the instructor.
7. After making the parts, file, drill, and sand as necessary.
8. Start assembling the robotics device. Make sure all parts are made and you are aware of the correct steps needed to complete the assembly.
9. Test the robot and make modifications.
10. Be ready to demonstrate and explain, in detail, your device.

## Conclusions

1. What is a robot?
2. What are the main parts of a robot?
3. What is an actuator?
4. What is the difference between hydraulics and pneumatics? Explain how each operates and/or functions.
5. If you were doing this activity over, what would you do differently?
6. What problems did you encounter and how did you solve them?
7. Explain the difference between a nonservo and servo robot. Which one is yours?
8. What is a manipulator and what are its four basic configurations?
9. Do you understand the role technology plays in the development of robotics? Explain your thoughts.

This activity adapted with permission from SPARKS: Activity Instructional Resource for Technology Education, Montgomery County Schools, Rockville, Maryland.

# Social Studies: Will It Pan Out?

## Purpose
To investigate one metal mined in the United States.

## Background
Janet and Matt have received a letter from their friend Steve. According to the letter, Steve has patented a revolutionary mining process that does not adversely affect the environment at all. Steve writes that his process can mine gold, silver, copper, or zinc from any ore without showing any traces on the land of mining that has occurred there.

This will make everyone involved very rich, Steve promises. But he needs partners with money to help him get started. He offers Janet and Matt what may be the opportunity of a lifetime. Is it? Steve writes that he can negotiate contracts with any land owner in the United States, government or private, because his process is so environmentally friendly. He wants you to see a demonstration of the process first; then you can all decide together where to mine and for what ore.

Janet and Matt are inclined to support Steve, but they do not want to give up all their savings until they do some research. They come to you and your group to ask for advice. They need you to answer some questions for them. Where are gold, silver, copper, and zinc are found in the United States? What is the history of each metal's price? What is the current price of each metal? How are these metals used?

Assuming Steve's process really does work, Janet and Matt will use your information to decide whether they should invest in such a mining operation and if so, what they should mine.

## Materials

**Per group of four:**
- Encyclopedias
- Research materials
- Atlas
- *Statistical Abstract of the United States*
- Construction and graph paper
- Colored pencils
- 4 outline maps of the United States
- Newspaper
- Discovery File "Gold, Silver, and Copper: What Are They Worth Today?" (page 41)

## Procedure
Conduct this activity in groups of four. Each member of the group will research one metal (gold, silver, copper, or zinc) and do the following tasks:
- Create a colored map of the United States that shows the states where the metal is found in sizable quantities.
- Create a line graph showing trends in the metal's price for the past 15 to 20 years. Use prices from the Discovery File on page 41. Mount the graph on construction paper.
- Create a line graph, mounted on construction paper, showing the price for the metal each day for the past week.
- Write a brief report on the properties of the metal that make it valuable, current uses of the metal, and the industries that rely on the metal.

After several class periods of researching and preparing visuals, report back to the group. As a group, decide (vote) which metal appears to have the brightest future and whether Janet and Matt should take Steve's offer.

Compare your group's decision with that of other groups and discuss the reasons for different conclusions.

# Math: The Best Fit

## Purpose

To determine a line or curve of best fit from which to estimate water pressure at various depths.

## Background

Minerals are found on dry land and in land that's under water. Either way, most minerals are found beneath the surface. Mining valuable minerals from under the oceans is certainly possible (see Discovery File "Harvesting the Ocean" on page 33), but it is costly. A big problem with underwater mining is water pressure. Water pressure increases rapidly with depth.

When real measurements are graphed, they rarely fall on a perfect line or curve. Errors in measurement and other variables cause data points to be scattered. When graphing real data, it is often better to draw a *line of best fit* rather than to connect all the points. In this activity, you will use a line of best fit to predict the pressure at various depths beneath the ocean surface.

## Materials

**Per student:**
- Data table of water pressure
- Graph paper

## Procedure

To construct a best-fit graph, begin by plotting all data points. Next draw a smooth line or curve that flows through most of the data points. The line does not have to touch all points.

For example, imagine dropping an object from a building. If you record in a table the distance the object has fallen at various times, you would get a table similar to this:

### A Freely Falling Object

| Time (in seconds) | Distance (in meters) |
|---|---|
| 0 | 0 |
| 1 | 5 |
| 2 | 20 |
| 3 | 44 |
| 4 | 79 |
| 5 | 123 |

You could graph these data and draw a best-fit curve to help estimate the distance the object will fall at other times.

Notice how the smooth curve does not pass through the center of every point. Predict how far the object would fall in six, seven, and eight seconds.

Here is a second example. A scientist is trying to find the relationship among when lightning is seen, when thunder is heard, and the distance the lightning is from the observer. She constructed the data table and best-fit line shown below.

### Lightning Strikes

| Time (in seconds) Between Thunder and Lightning | Distance (in miles) Between Thunder and Lightning |
|---|---|
| 1 | 0.2 |
| 2 | 0.3 |
| 3 | 0.5 |
| 4 | 0.7 |

Predict how far lightning is from the observer if the thunder is 5, 6, or 10 seconds later.

Use the data below to construct a line or curve of best fit.

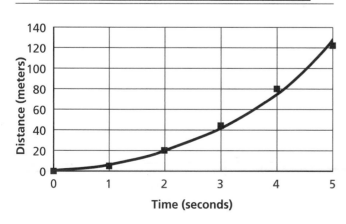

A Freely Falling Object

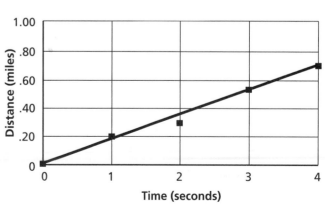

Lightning Strikes

Then use the best-fit graph to estimate water pressure at various other depths. At what depth do you believe a diver would be in danger? Why?

| Table of Water Pressure | |
| --- | --- |
| Depth (in Feet) | Pressure (in Pounds per Square Inch) |
| 10 | 4.4 |
| 20 | 9.0 |
| 40 | 17.0 |
| 60 | 26.0 |
| 80 | 35.0 |
| 100 | 44.0 |

## Extension

Find other data tables in science and try to find a best-fit line or curve for them.

# Writing to Persuade

## Purpose

To demonstrate knowledge of appropriate science concepts and the persuasive writing style in an editorial about the renewal of the Mining Law of 1872.

## Background

Occasionally, laws must be renewed by Congress. Imagine the 1872 Mining Law is one such law that will be coming up for examination in the coming year. Read the Discovery File "Mining Law" on page 29. You may also want to read the articles on the law in the module and other information you can find. As you read, you should begin to form an opinion about whether the law should be renewed.

## Materials

**Per student:**

- Discovery File "Mining Law" (page 29)

- Copy of Peer-Response Form (page 55)

- Proofreading Guidesheet (page 56)

- Reference materials on Mining Law of 1872

## Procedure

Imagine you are the editor of a newspaper. Write an editorial about the Mining Law of 1872. State your position on the renewal or modification of that act. Try to persuade your readers to agree with you.

Begin with an introduction that gets your readers' attention. Be sure to explain the law—its history and its effects. Clearly state your opinion about its re-

newal. Most importantly, use facts and data from pages in this module to support your opinion. Finally, write a conclusion that sums up your opinion.

An exceptional editorial:

- Has an attention-getting introduction.

- Clearly states an opinion.

- Gives factual background.

- Uses data and facts to support the opinion.

- Has a strong conclusion.

- Is relatively error-free and follows conventions of grammar.

Use the Proofreading Guidesheet on page 56 to edit your editorial. Have your peers evaluate and react to your letter using a copy of the Peer-Response Form on page 55.

## Questions

1. How do you get your readers' attention?
2. How and where is your opinion clearly stated?
3. What information about the Mining Law of 1872 do you include? What other information might you include?
4. What data and facts do you use about the law to support your opinion?
5. What other data might you use?
6. How could you improve your conclusion to make it stronger?

# Peer-Response Form

**Directions**

1. Ask your partners to listen carefully as you read your rough draft aloud.

2. Ask your partners to help you improve your writing by telling you their answers to the questions below.

3. Jot down notes about what your partners say:

   a. What did you like best about my rough draft?

   b. What did you have the hardest time understanding about my rough draft?

   c. What can you suggest that I do to improve my rough draft?

4. Exchange rough drafts with a partner. In pencil, place a check mark near any mechanical, spelling, or grammatical constructions about which you are uncertain. Return the papers and check your own. Ask your partner for clarification if you do not understand or agree with the comments on your paper. Jot down notes you want to remember when writing your revision.

# Proofreading Guidesheet

1. Have you identified the assigned purpose of the writing assignment? Have you accomplished this purpose?

2. Have you written on the assigned topic?

3. Have you identified the assigned form your writing should take? Have you written accordingly?

4. Have you addressed the assigned audience?

5. Have you used sentences of different lengths and types to make your writing effective?

6. Have you chosen language carefully so the reader understands what you mean?

7. Have you done the following to make your writing clear for someone else to read?
   - used appropriate capitalization
   - kept pronouns clear
   - kept verb tense consistent
   - used correct spelling
   - used correct punctuation
   - used complete sentences
   - made all subjects and verbs agree
   - organized your ideas into logical paragraphs

## Books

Arem, Joel. *Rocks and Minerals.* Phoenix: Geoscience Press, Inc., 1991.

Chesterman, Charles W. (contributor). *Familiar Rocks and Minerals of North America.* New York: Alfred A. Knopf, 1988.

Pough, Frederick H. *A Field Guide to Rocks and Minerals* (The Peterson Field Guide Series). Boston: Houghton Mifflin Company, 1995.

Schumann, Walter. *Minerals of the World.* New York: Sterling Publishing Co., Inc., 1992.

## Organizations

Arizona Mining Association
#2702 North Third Street, Suite 2015
Phoenix, AZ 85004
Director of Education: Dr. Larry McBiles

The Gold Institute and The Silver Institute
1112 16th Street N.W., Suite 240
Washington, DC 20036

Mineral Policy Center
1612 K Street N.W., Suite 808
Washington, DC 20006
Mineral Policy Center provides information, publications, films, and videotapes on the environmental impacts of mineral development. Members receive their "Clementine" and publications including *Burden of Gilt,* which is on the legacy of environmental damage from abandoned mines

and what America should do about it. Videotapes are loaned to members. Titles include *Abandoned Mines, The New Gold Rush,* and *Poison in the Rockies.* Membership is $25 per year.

The Wilderness Society
900 17th Street N.W.
Washington, DC 20006-2596
Published "Undermining America: The 1872 Mining Law," a four-page fact sheet from 1993, and "Restoring Environmental Leadership: A Public Lands Agenda for the '90s."

## Government Agencies

For publications below, write to:
Superintendent of Documents
Government Printing Office
Washington, DC 20402-9371

*Bureau of Mines: The Minerals Source* (brochure) and *Minerals Today* (Bureau of Mines magazine) are published by the U.S. Bureau of Mines, Department of the Interior. Cost is $13 for six issues.

The U.S. Geological Survey, Department of the Interior, publishes these brochures: *Natural Gemstones, Geologic Time, Gold, Prospecting for Gold,* and *Suggestions for Prospecting.*

## Magazines and Publications

*Gold Prospector: The Magazine of Mining and Adventure*
Gold Prospectors Association of America

P.O. Box 891509
Temecula, CA 92589-1509
Membership with bimonthly magazine is $30 per year; magazine only is $15 for the six issues per year.

*Rocks & Minerals*
4000 Albemarle Street N.W.
Washington, DC 20016
(800) 365-9753
Cost is $28 per year for six issues. Single-issue cost is $7.50.

*The Mining Record*
5660 Greenwood Plaza Blvd., Suite 450
Englewood, CO 80111
(800) 441-4748

*International Mining News*
This has been the industry's leading weekly mining newspaper since 1889. Cost is $1 per copy or $39 per year.

*Earth Magazine*
Find this on a newsstand or call (800) 533-6644.

*The Klondike Stampede of 1897–1898,* a special issue of *Cobblestone Magazine* (the history magazine for young people), Vol. 1, No. 8, August 1980.

*The Glory of Gold,* a special issue of *Faces Magazine* (the magazine about people), Vol. VI, No. III, December 1989.

# ACKNOWLEDGMENTS

## Author
Russell G. Wright, with contributions from Barbara Sprungman, Leonard David, and the following teachers:
Charles Doebler, Robert Frost Middle School, Rockville, Maryland
Nell Jeter, Earle B. Wood Middle School, Rockville, Maryland
Richard Knight, Baker Middle School, Damascus, Maryland
William R. Krayer, Gaithersburg High School, Gaithersburg, Maryland
Robert McDowell, Albert Einstein High School, Kensington, Maryland
Eugene M. Molesky, Ridgeview Middle School, Gaithersburg, Maryland
Sheila Shillinger, Montgomery Village Middle School, Gaithersburg, Maryland
Thomas Smith, Briggs Chaney Middle School, Silver Spring, Maryland

## Science Activities
Nancy Carey, Col. E. Brooke Lee Middle School, Silver Spring, Maryland
Frank S. Weisel, Poolesville Junior/Senior High School, Poolesville, Maryland.

## Interdisciplinary Activities
Bernard Hudock, Watkins Mill High School, Gaithersburg, Maryland
Jeanne S. Klugel, John F. Kennedy High School, Silver Spring, Maryland
Joseph Panarella, Montgomery Village Middle School, Gaithersburg, Maryland
John Senuta, Ridgeview Middle School, Gaithersburg, Maryland

## Teacher-Writer Interns
Kelly Hortch, University of Maryland, College Park, Maryland

Donna Obermeier, University of Maryland, College Park, Maryland

## Geology Advisor
Evan Wolff, Northern Arizona University, Flagstaff, Arizona

## Scientific Reviewers
Roger Ashley, United States Geological Survey
Dave Davidson, United States Geological Survey
Dorothy K. Hall, National Aeronautics and Space Administration

## Student Consultants
Col. E. Brooke Lee Middle School, Silver Spring, Maryland: Sherri Blase, Brianne Carey, Kelley Legge, Shatish Moore, Justin Nero, Koya Reams, Jamii Steward, John Sustar, Alfred Wagna, Russell Williams

## Field-Test Teachers
Judith Basile, Agawam Junior High School, Feeding Hills, Massachusetts
Mark Carlson, Westlane Middle School, Indianapolis, Indiana
Adrianne Criminger, Lanier Middle School, Buford, Georgia
Kevin Feeney, Northeast Middle Middle School, Baltimore, Maryland
Cheryl Glotfelty, Northern Middle School, Accident, Maryland
Linda Mosser, Northern Middle School, Accident, Maryland
David Needham, Albert Einstein Middle School, Sacramento, California
Amy Resler, Westlane Middle School, Indianapolis, Indiana
Karen Shugrue, Agawam Junior High School, Feeding Hills, Massachusetts

Gloria Yost, Albert Einstein Middle School, Sacramento, California

## EBS Advisory Committee
Dr. Eddie Anderson, National Aeronautic and Space Administration
Ms. Mary Ann Brearton, American Association for the Advancement of Science
Dr. Lynn Dierking, Science Learning, Inc.
Mr. Bob Dubill, *USA Today*
Mr. Herbert Freiberger, United States Geological Survey
Ms. Joyce Gross, National Oceanic and Atmospheric Administration
Dr. Harry Herzer, National Aeronautic and Space Administration
Dr. Frank Ireton, American Geophysical Union
Mr. Bill Krayer, Gaithersburg High School
Dr. Rocky Lopes, American Red Cross
Dr. Jerry Lynch, John T. Baker Middle School
Ms. Marilyn P. MacCabe, Federal Emergency Management Agency
Ms. Virginia Major, United States Geological Survey
Mr. John Ortman, United States Department of Energy
Dr. Noel Raufasté, Jr., National Institute of Standards and Technology
Dr. Bill Sacco, Trianalytics Corporation
Mr. Ron Slotkin, United States Environmental Protection Agency
Ms. Linda Straka, Federal Emergency Management Agency